NATURAL WORLD

EYEWITNESS

NATURAL WORLD

Written by
STEVE PARKER

DORLING KINDERSLEY
London • New York • Munich • Melbourne • Delhi

LONDON, NEW YORK, MUNICH,
MELBOURNE, and DELHI

Senior editor Louise Pritchard
Senior art editor Jill Plank
Project editor Djinn von Noorden
Art editor Sharon Spencer
Designers Ivan Finnegan, Kati Poynor
Managing editor Simon Adams
Managing art editor Julia Harris
Production Catherine Semark

First published in Great Britain in 1995 by
Dorling Kindersley Limited,
80 Strand, London WC2R 0RL

2 4 6 8 10 9 7 5 3 1

Copyright © 1994
Dorling Kindersley Limited, London
This edition Published 2002

A CIP catalogue record for this book is
available from the British Library.

ISBN 0 7513 6050 3

Colour reproduction by
Colourscan, Singapore
Printed and bound in Hong Kong/China
by South China Printing Co.

See our complete product line at
www.dk.com

CONTENTS

FOREWORD

LIFE EXISTS IN MANY FORMS. There are about 4,000,000 known species of plants and animals living today, and most people encounter only a few of them. But through photographs in books, and films on television, we all have an opportunity to study the incredible array of living things with which we share our planet. Often, we are surprised: some animals appear bizarre, while others seem extravagant in their use of colours and decorations. But Nature does not view them that way. Their extraordinary looks and vivid colours are strictly functional. The tiger's striped coat was not designed by chance, but evolved as camouflage. The pattern enables this hunter to blend in with its forest home and ambush its unsuspecting victims. Isolate the tiger from its natural surroundings and place it in a world of white, and at once its beautiful coat and powerful frame are revealed for what they are. What is more, the animal seems to leap right off the page. This is Eyewitness.

PHOTOGRAPHIC TECHNIQUES

Specialist close-up lenses provide us with a new view of the familiar, revealing such detail that we can learn more about each plant and animal subject and so appreciate it all the more. High-speed photography freezes rapid movement, while time-lapse techniques enable us to experience the passage of time. Together these remarkable methods bring to us the action and drama in the living world. Photography is also a means by which new discoveries can be recorded. Discoveries need no longer be suspected as figments of an explorer's imagination. We can now have photographic proof of genuine scientific bombshells. We may not have believable pictures of the Loch Ness monster or the yeti, but we do have photographs of the okapi, discovered for science in 1901, and the megamouth shark, lifted accidentally from the deep Pacific in 1976, and a whole lot more.

MAKING NEW DISCOVERIES

Photographers and film makers can make new discoveries themselves. A team in Borneo, for example, once chanced upon a small nondescript frog which, quite unexpectedly, waved a bright-blue foot in the air. A photographer was there to record the event and in doing so presented the scientific community with a brand new species of frog. It lives beside a waterfall where normal froggy sounds are drowned by the roar of the water. So the curious creature communicates with its fellow frogs by shaking a leg. Scientists chance upon previously undiscovered species of plants and animals almost daily – in rainforests, grasslands, deserts, on the top of mountains, and in the depths of the sea. It is disturbing to realize that by destroying rainforests and by polluting the seas we are losing plants and animals without even knowing that they are there. Films and photographs help us to keep a permanent record of the plants and animals we know, and Eyewitness is contributing to this audit of life on Earth.

Michael Bright

Managing Editor
Wildvision
BBC Natural History Unit

CHAPTER 1

FORM & FUNCTION

An animal's size, shape, and design provide many clues about its food, habits, way of life, and the group to which it belongs. The form and structure of the millions of different creatures in the animal kingdom, which range from tiny ants to enormous elephants, are invariably adapted to their particular functions and lifestyle.

MANY SLIMY ARMS
Unlike human limbs, the tentacles of the common octopus have no stiff bones in them. Its rubbery, flexible flesh suits its shy and stealthy lifestyle. The octopus spends much of its time squeezed into caves or crevices, where it lurks in wait and grabs crabs, fish, and shellfish as they pass by.

CLINGING FOR A LIVING
This treefrog from Belize is perfectly adapted to its rainforest home. It clings to the smooth leaves, slippery twigs, and shiny vines with sucker-like discs on its fingers and toes. The treefrog peers through the gloom between the dripping trees with its huge eyes, watching for food. As flies, moths, and beetles fly past, the frog catches them and swallows them whole.

Hard-wearing parts

MOST ANIMALS have hard parts somewhere in or on their body. Some, such as mammals, and including humans, bats, and lions have a bony internal skeleton, called an endoskeleton, as support; others, such as insects, spiders, shellfish, and other invertebrates have an outside skeleton, or exoskeleton. Some animals, such as lobsters, tortoises, and turtles, have a hard shell. The type and design of shell depends on the animal group from which the creature comes. These shells are from very different kinds of animals.

A RIGID CASE
The tortoise above and the turtle below are both reptiles. Their shells are made of plates of bone. Inside the shell, and fused to it at various sites, are the usual skeleton bones.

Special hairs called setae help the crab to find its way around. They also detect the movements of predators or food in the water

Upper carapace covers back of turtle

Lower plastron covers belly

A STIFF BAG
The land tortoise and the river turtle have the same basic shell, but the differing details indicate their contrasting habitats and lifestyles. The river turtle's shell is not quite so hard, heavy, and rigid as that of the tortoise. Its curved plates of bone have large air spaces in them, for lightness. This helps the turtle to swim in mid water and near the surface, rather than sinking like a stone to the bottom. The horny outer plates which cover the tortoise's shell are absent, and the whole shell has a more streamlined shape for faster movement. Tortoises are not noted for their speed. But the river turtle can swim quite swiftly using its powerful, paddle-shaped limbs.

AN ALL-OVER SHELL

Molluscs, such as the snail, have the most complete, wraparound shells of almost any animal. The shell is rigid and unjointed, unlike the body casing of the crab below. The snail can withdraw completely into its shell. When danger passes, it cautiously emerges and moves on.

A tough operculum protects the shell opening

The foot is the first part to emerge

Body muscles pull the shell up and over for better protection

The head begins to appear, and tentacles test the air for smells

Muscles pull the shell into the travelling position off the ground

The body is extended and the snail slides off on its slimy foot

Feathery mouthparts for feeding

ONE SHELL IN ANOTHER

The hermit crab belongs to the animal group called crustaceans. These have a jointed shell – an outer body casing called an exoskeleton, which is jointed to allow movement. The joints can be seen most clearly on the pincers and legs. The hermit crab is unusual among crustaceans in that the back part of its body is not armoured. So the crab reverses into an empty mollusc shell, in this case a conch, and uses the shell to protect its soft rear end. As the crab moults its body casing and grows a new, larger one, it must also find a new, larger shell.

Joint in exoskeleton allows pincer to move

Crab can back almost completely into its second-hand shell and block the opening with its large claws

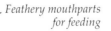

Under the skin

Under an animal's fur, feathers, scales, skin, or shell, are the soft, fleshy bits – such as muscles, guts, nerves, and blood vessels. Apart from a few very simple animals, such as sponges and jellyfish, most creatures have the same basic set of main internal parts, called organs. There is a digestive tube incorporating a stomach and intestines; muscles for movement; a blood system to transport food and oxygen around the body; a waste-disposal system; sense organs such as eyes to detect what is going on; and nerves and a brain to make sure everything works together.

This siphon squirts out waste products; a small siphon at the other end allows water to pass into the body

MUSCLE POWER
Most animal movements are based on muscles. The dog leaps using more than 500 body muscles. Each shortens, or contracts, for a precise time to give a smooth, coordinated jump. The clam clamps closed using fewer than 10 muscles. Yet these can hold the two valves of its shell shut together for many hours.

LOVELY LIPS
The "lips" of the giant blue clam are its mantle, the fleshy wraparound part that covers its body and lines its shell. The mantle is sensitive to touch and chemicals. It also has rows of simple eyes. The green patches are algae (microscopic plants). They grow naturally in the clam's flesh.

When the clam closes, the ridges and lumps on its shell disguise it as an old rock

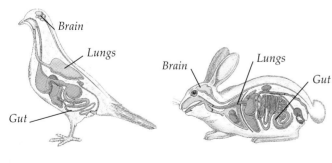

Brain

Lungs

Gut

Brain

Lungs

Gut

INTERNAL DESIGN
Despite the different shapes and layouts, the rabbit and the pigeon have the same basic set of internal organs. The brain is in the head, the lungs are in the chest, and the long gut squiggles through the rear part of the body. Similarity in internal design shows an evolutionary relationship.

At each stage of the dog's leap, many muscles are making sure that the animal is well balanced. The strong muscles of the hips and back legs push hard on take-off. The head and tail shift position for control and balance in mid air. The front legs extend to take the force of the landing. Even as it curves through the air, the dog is alert and keeps looking and listening. The leap is the natural movement when a dog pounces on its prey.

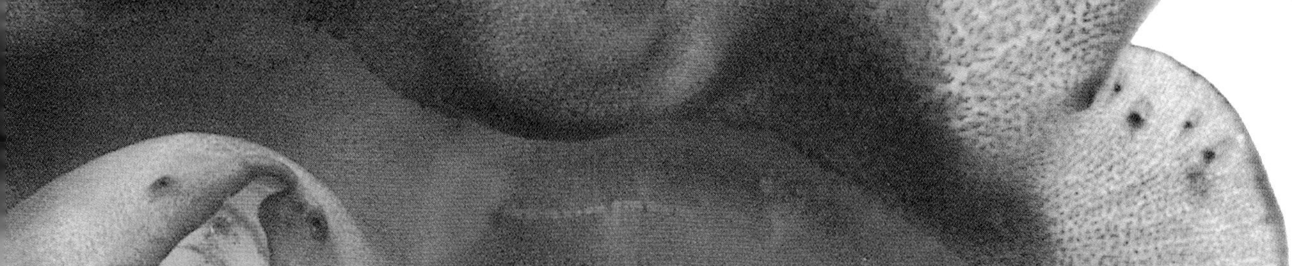

Simple eyes

Algae catch sunlight for energy and make nutrients, which the clam uses. In return, the clam gives these tiny plants a safe home

19

The parts of an insect

INSECTS MAKE UP by far the largest group of animals, with more than one million different species. A typical insect has three main body sections: the head with mouthparts and antennae; the thorax with six legs and (usually) wings; and the abdomen. These are encased in a hard external skeleton composed largely of a tough, horny substance called chitin. This exoskeleton covers all parts of the body including the legs, feet, eyes, antennae, and even the internal breathing tubes, or tracheae. Young insects have to shed their exoskeleton, or moult, several times during their lives in order to grow to adult size.

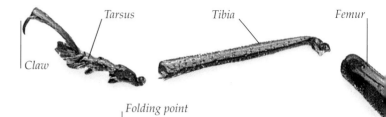

Tarsus

Claw

Tibia

Femur

Folding point

Front, or leading edge of wing

Tip, or apex, of wing

Base of wing folds underneath

HIND WING FOLDED
In order to fit beneath the wing cases, the larger hind wings, with which the beetle flies, must be folded. The wing tip, or apex, is folded back at a special break in the front, known as the folding point. The base of the wing is also folded underneath.

JEWEL BEETLE
This adult jewel beetle, shown here at over three times life size, comes from South America. Beetles are the largest subgroup of insects, with more than 250,000 species. They have the typical jointed legs possessed by all insects.

ABDOMEN
The abdomen of an insect contains most of its "maintenance equipment" – the digestive system, heart, and sexual organs. Like the other parts of the body it is protected by the rigid exoskeleton. But between the segments the body is flexible. The whole surface is covered by a thin layer of wax which prevents the insect from losing too much water.

INTERNAL ANATOMY
This illustration shows the internal anatomy of a typical insect – a worker bee. Along the centre of its body is the digestive system (yellow), which is a continuous tube divided into the foregut, midgut, and hindgut. The breathing, or respiratory, system (white) consists of a network of branched tubes, through which air passes from the spiracles to every part of the body. The two large air sacs in the abdomen are important for supplying the flight muscles in the thorax with air. The bee's heart is a long thin tube, which pumps blood along most of the upper part of the body. There are no other blood vessels. Blood leaves the heart to carry food to the other organs. The simple nervous system (blue) is formed by one main nerve, which has knots of massed nerve cells, or ganglia, along its length. The ganglion in the head is the insect's brain. The female sexual organs and store of poison leading to the sting are shown in green.

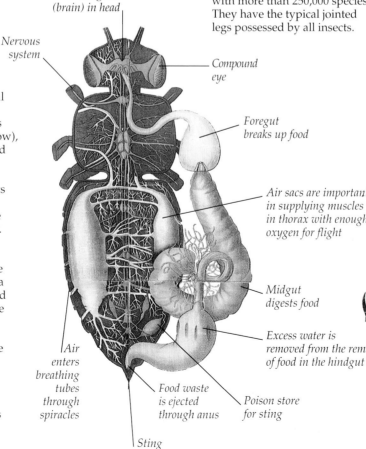

Ganglion (brain) in head

Nervous system

Compound eye

Foregut breaks up food

Air sacs are important in supplying muscles in thorax with enough oxygen for flight

Midgut digests food

Excess water is removed from the remains of food in the hindgut

Air enters breathing tubes through spiracles

Food waste is ejected through anus

Poison store for sting

Sting

FRONT WING
In beetles, the front pair of wings is adapted as a pair of hard wing cases called elytra. These protect the delicate flying wings and the body, and are often brightly coloured. When the beetle flies, they are held forward.

LEGS

Insects have three pairs of jointed legs, which are used for walking, running, or jumping – depending on the species. Each leg has four main parts. The coxa joins the leg to the thorax. The femur, or thigh, is the most muscular section of the leg. The tibia, or lower leg, often carries a number of spines for self defence. The tarsus, the equivalent of a human foot, consists of between one and five segments and two claws between which is sometimes a small pad for gripping smooth surfaces.

ARMOUR PLATING

A tank is like a large beetle, with its hard outer skin protecting the important inner workings from being damaged by enemies.

Tarsus has between one and five segments

Tibia

Femur

Coxa

Second and third segments of the thorax each bear a pair of wings and a pair of legs

Coxa

Each foot bears two claws for climbing on rough surfaces

FEEDING IN INFORMATION

The head carries the feeding apparatus as well as important sense organs such as the compound eyes, antennae, and the palps, or feelers. These are attached to the mouthparts and help give the insect information about the taste and smell of its food.

ANTENNAE

The antennae, or "feelers", of insects vary in size and shape from long and thin, as in crickets, to short and hair-like, as in some flies. But whatever their shape, the antennae bear sensory structures that are able to detect air movements, vibrations, and smells.

Compound eye

COMPOUND EYES

Insect eyes are called compound because each is made up of hundreds of tiny, simple eyes. These eyes enable an insect to detect movement around it in almost every direction at once.

First segment of thorax bears front pair of legs

THORAX

The thorax is made up of three segments. The first bears the first pair of legs and is often clearly separated from the second and third segments, each of which has a pair of wings and a pair of legs. The second and third segments are closely joined to the abdomen.

Segmented antenna detects vibrations and smells

Leading edge of hind wing

A spiracle can be closed to prevent the entry of air and control water loss

Claw

HIND WING OUTSTRETCHED

The wings have no muscles in them. As the wing cases are lifted, muscles inside the thorax pull on the leading edge of the hind wings, making them open automatically and then flick up and down.

Wing case, or elytron

A BREATH OF FRESH AIR

Insects breathe air through a network of tubes (tracheae), that extend into the body from pairs of openings in the cuticle called spiracles. Some insects, like this caterpillar, have a pair of spiracles on each segment. More active insects often have fewer spiracles, as they can force air out of the tracheae.

Life in a shell

THE MOLLUSCS ARE ONE OF THE LARGEST of all animal groups, with about 100,000 species. They include creatures commonly called shellfish, such as oysters, mussels, whelks, and cockles. Also in the mollusc group are slugs and snails, limpets and conches, and nautilus, cuttlefish, squid, and octopuses. Most molluscs live in the sea, and most have a hard, lime-rich shell to protect their soft body. The shell is manufactured by the fleshy mantle, which encloses the various body organs on the inside.

ROCOCO DECORATION
The beautiful forms of mollusc shells have inspired countless artists and architects throughout the centuries. Here, the radiating shape of a clam shell has been used to decorate an arched recess.

LIVING IN A WHORL
The nautilus is a sea mollusc related to octopuses and cuttlefish. This is its shell, cut in half to reveal the complex inner architecture. The animal itself lives in the largest chamber. It has two large eyes and about 30 tentacles which it uses to seize prey.

Most recent living chamber

Edge of chamber

Buoyancy chambers

Cross-section of nautilus shell

Shell mouth, or opening

Lip of shell

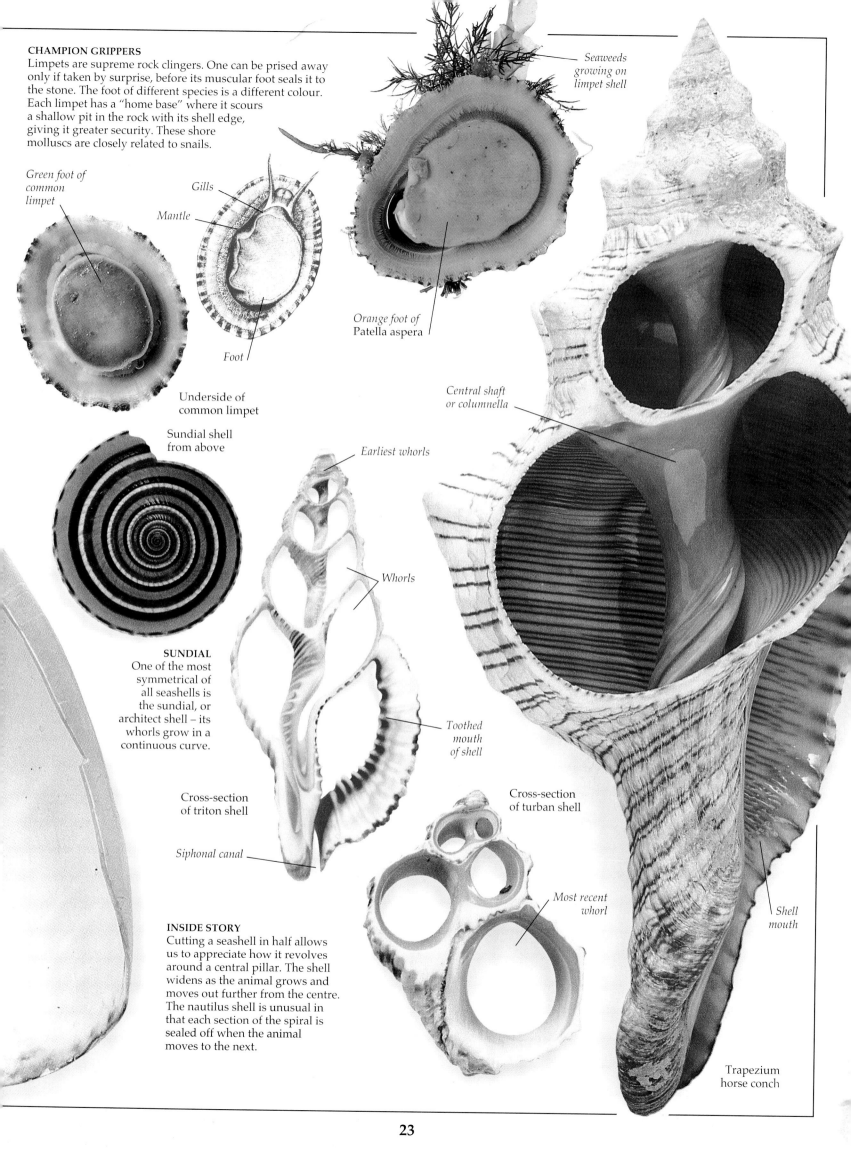

CHAMPION GRIPPERS

Limpets are supreme rock clingers. One can be prised away only if taken by surprise, before its muscular foot seals it to the stone. The foot of different species is a different colour. Each limpet has a "home base" where it scours a shallow pit in the rock with its shell edge, giving it greater security. These shore molluscs are closely related to snails.

Green foot of common limpet

Gills

Mantle

Foot

Seaweeds growing on limpet shell

Orange foot of Patella aspera

Underside of common limpet

Sundial shell from above

Central shaft or columnella

Earliest whorls

Whorls

SUNDIAL
One of the most symmetrical of all seashells is the sundial, or architect shell – its whorls grow in a continuous curve.

Toothed mouth of shell

Cross-section of triton shell

Cross-section of turban shell

Siphonal canal

Most recent whorl

INSIDE STORY
Cutting a seashell in half allows us to appreciate how it revolves around a central pillar. The shell widens as the animal grows and moves out further from the centre. The nautilus shell is unusual in that each section of the spiral is sealed off when the animal moves to the next.

Shell mouth

Trapezium horse conch

Circular animals

IN NEARLY ALL the major animal groups, from worms to mammals, the basic body plan is bilateral symmetry – that is, one side of their body is a mirror image of the other. The glaring exception is the echinoderms, or "spiny skins". This animal group has radial symmetry – a circular body plan. Echinoderms include the many kinds of starfish, brittlestars, and sea urchins, and the less familiar forms such as sea cucumbers, sea lilies, and feather stars. All the 6,000-plus species of echinoderms live only in the oceans, many of them in deep water. The closest most people get to them is on the seashore.

GETTING A GRIP
When handled, starfish are rigid and resistant. However, the flexibility of their arms is shown when a wave flips them over: the arm tips curl under, the tiny tube feet get a grip on the rock, and slowly the animal rights itself.

Starfish have suckers on their tube feet which help them to grip on to rocks

A BALL WITH FIVE ARMS
The sea urchin, like the starfish, has five rays or "arms", as this underside view shows. An urchin is like a starfish whose arms have curled up and come together over its centre, making a ball. The long tilting spines give protection. The thin tube feet grip the rock, seize food, and throw off debris.

Mouth (Aristotle's lantern)

Anchoring tube feet

Holes where tube feet passed through

Tube feet searching water

Underside of common sea urchin

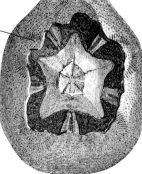

THE INNER URCHIN
Without spines and skin, the test (inner shell) of the sea urchin is revealed.

UNDERNEATH THE STARFISH

A starfish has no proper head or brain. Its control centre is a ring of nerves with branches into each arm. These control the movements of hundreds of waving tube feet. Each tube is a flexible finger-shaped sac, pumped full of body fluid and flexed by tiny muscles. The mouth is in the centre of the underside of the animal. Starfish are great hunters, and will eat mussels, clams, and similar shellfish.

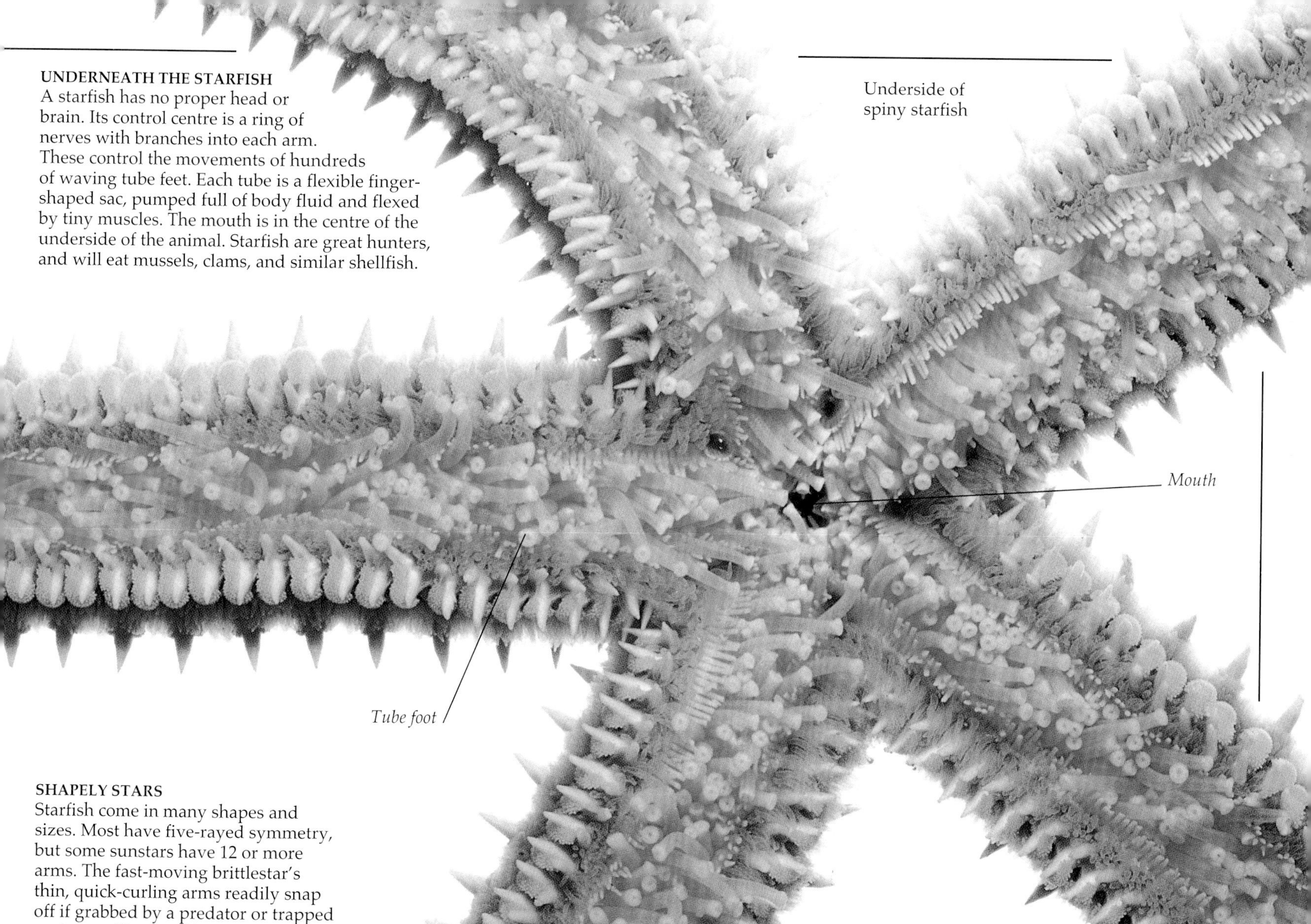

Underside of spiny starfish

Mouth

Tube foot

SHAPELY STARS

Starfish come in many shapes and sizes. Most have five-rayed symmetry, but some sunstars have 12 or more arms. The fast-moving brittlestar's thin, quick-curling arms readily snap off if grabbed by a predator or trapped under a rolling boulder. But losing an arm isn't a problem – the animal soon grows another one.

Spines are part of the spiny starfish skeleton

Common brittlestar

Cushion stars

Spiny starfish (upper side)

Crusty crustaceans

OFTEN CALLED SHELLFISH, crustaceans are neither true fish, nor do they have true shells, like molluscs. The hard outer body casing of a crustacean is jointed and gives all-over protection. This exoskeleton, similar to the hard outer casing of an insect's body, is made mainly of a limey substance and the protein chitin. There are many other similarities between crustaceans and insects, including segmented bodies and jointed limbs, and the shedding of its exoskeleton to allow the animal to grow. There are more than 30,000 species of crustaceans, and the vast majority live in the sea. They range from tiny daphnias and woodlice to sandhoppers, barnacles, krill, shrimps, prawns, and spindly spider crabs with legs almost three metres long. The massive armoured lobster, here shown slightly larger than life-size, is also a crustacean.

Still Life with Lobster by Joris Van Son

Tailpiece or telson

Abdomen is divided into six segments, or somites

STRONG WHEN INTACT
Because of the way in which the segments of its body are joined together, a lobster can swim only backwards or forwards – it cannot twist sideways. The shelly somites are made from chitin, which is strengthened by deposits of calcium salts. The somites are much softer at the joints, to allow the animal to move about. In order to grow, the lobster must occasionally shed its exoskeleton and grow a new one. This makes it extremely vulnerable to predators, and the lobster wisely hides away until its new casing has had time to harden.

COPYCAT CASING
Like the knights of old, crustaceans such as lobsters and crabs sacrificed flexibility in return for a protective suit of armour.

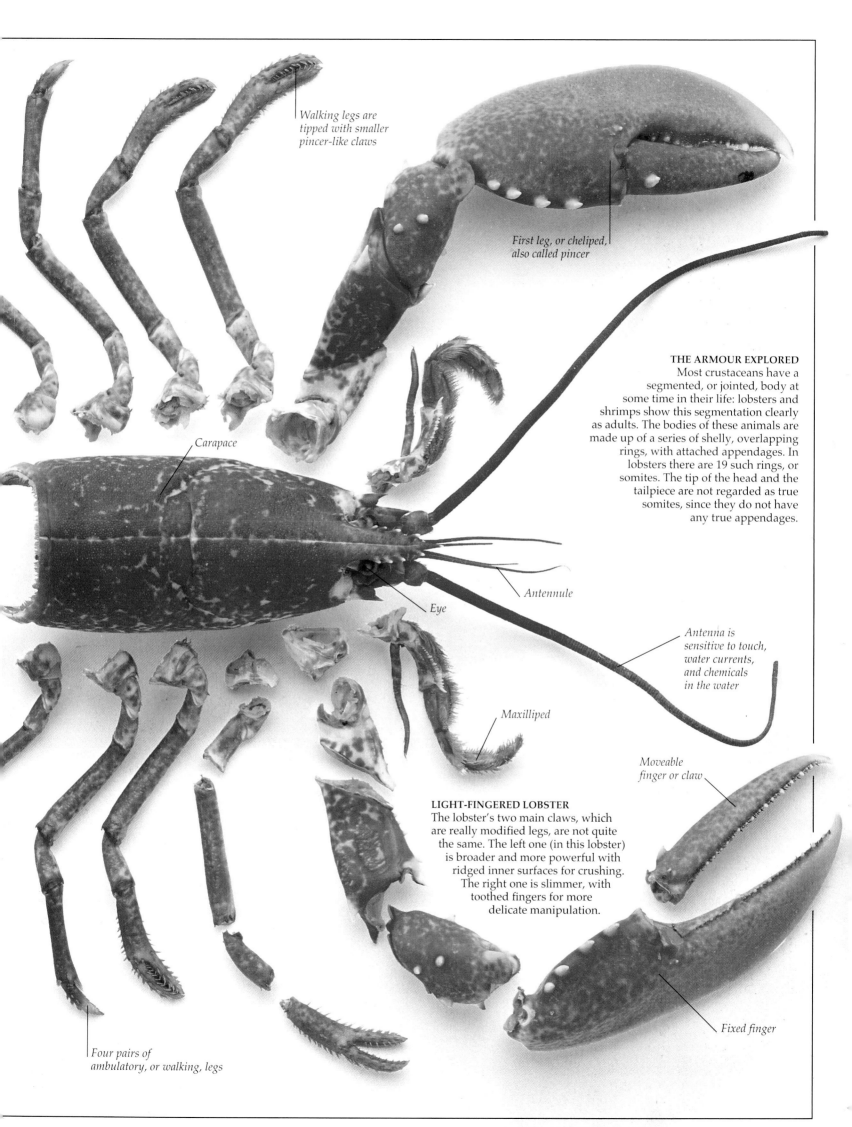

Walking legs are tipped with smaller pincer-like claws

First leg, or cheliped, also called pincer

Carapace

THE ARMOUR EXPLORED
Most crustaceans have a segmented, or jointed, body at some time in their life: lobsters and shrimps show this segmentation clearly as adults. The bodies of these animals are made up of a series of shelly, overlapping rings, with attached appendages. In lobsters there are 19 such rings, or somites. The tip of the head and the tailpiece are not regarded as true somites, since they do not have any true appendages.

Antennule

Antenna is sensitive to touch, water currents, and chemicals in the water

Eye

Maxilliped

Moveable finger or claw

LIGHT-FINGERED LOBSTER
The lobster's two main claws, which are really modified legs, are not quite the same. The left one (in this lobster) is broader and more powerful with ridged inner surfaces for crushing. The right one is slimmer, with toothed fingers for more delicate manipulation.

Four pairs of ambulatory, or walking, legs

Fixed finger

Masters of the watery world

Fish were the first vertebrates (animals with backbones), and the ancestors of the first land-dwelling vertebrates, the amphibians. There are more than 21,000 species of fish, from tiny pygmy gobies to sharks larger than a juggernaut truck. The typical fish's body is built around its internal framework of bones, called the endoskeleton. Blocks of muscles along either side of the body pull on the backbone to swish the tail from side to side, so the fish can swim. A fish takes in oxygen from the water through its gills, feathery blood-rich structures just behind the eyes.

First dorsal fin

Cranium supports and protects the brain

Eye socket

Upper jaw

Lower jaw

Atlantic cod

Opercular bones form the gill covers and protect the delicate gills

Heart, stomach, and other internal organs are in this region

Pectoral fin

Interhaemals support fin along the underside

Pelvic fins – in the cod, these are in front of the pectorals

A LOAD OF OLD BONES
This well-preserved skeleton of an Atlantic cod is typical of the great majority of teleosts, or "true" bony fish. Like most successful groups of animals, fish have evolved into various shapes and sizes in order to cope with different lifestyles. The shape of the internal skeleton changes accordingly. Portions may increase in size to support and enlarge part of the body, or shrink away to almost nothing when their framework and rigidity are no longer needed.

BASKER'S BACKBONE
The basking shark is the world's second-largest fish, after the whale shark. Being a shark, its skeleton is made mainly of cartilage. This is the central portion or centrum of a vertebra, strengthened by a network of mineral-laced fibres.

Dorsal fin is toward the end of the body

TRUNKFISH TRUNK
The trunkfish's backbone has long supporting rods for its dorsal fin, which is not in the middle of the body but near the tail. This fish's body is covered in a protective box of "chain mail", formed from bony scales. It swims slowly with its fins and tail, since its body is too stiff to flex, or bend, in the normal way.

Trunkfish

STOUT, NOT SPEEDY
The backbone of the cascadura, a South American armoured catfish, is stout and inflexible. This fish has rows of overlapping bony plates along its body, sacrificing speed for armoured protection.

FISH SCALES

Fish like this rudd have a body covering of large scales. A scale grows from the skin along one of its sides, the other sides being free. It is made of a thin, semi-transparent, bone-like substance. The scales overlap like tiles on a roof. Some fish, such as eels and catfish, have tiny scales; some have none at all.

Rudd

Interneurals - support the fins along the back

Second dorsal fin – unlike many fish, the cod has three dorsal fins

Spine

Blocks of muscle lie alongside the spine

EVERGREEN BONES

Marine garfish are often caught by anglers. But people are put off eating them by the strange bright green colour of the skeleton. No one knows why garfish have green bones – the colour lasts even after boiling.

Marine garfish

Lepidotrichs, or fin rays support all dorsal and anal fins

Caudal fin (tail)

Front anal fin – unlike many fish, the cod has two anal fins

Rear anal fin

Tail vertebrae

ARTHRITIC FISH

As the spadefish ages, it tends to develop thickenings on its bones and fin rays, called hyperosteosis. Affected fish seem to live fairly normally, even though their skulls and fins can become grotesquely swollen. No one is quite sure why the swellings occur. It may be that minerals such as calcium build up in the body, from the fish's coral-munching habits.

CURVED CENTRUM

In most bony fish the centrum (central portion) of the vertebra is dished, or concave, as in the pike. But in the freshwater gar, the centrum is projecting or convex.

Convex centrum of freshwater gar

Concave centrum of pike

Sailfish

Vertebrae showing characteristic swelling from bone disease

OPEN-OCEAN SAILOR

Great oceanic fish have immensely powerful muscles, and need a strong backbone to match. This is a vertebra from a sailfish, one of the fastest swimmers, showing the large projecting flanges for stability and muscle anchorage. A sailfish can reach speeds of up to 100 km/h (over 60 mph).

Large projecting flanges

WAGGING TAIL

The rearmost vertebrae from a trunkfish (see far left) have keels for muscle attachment. The tail is flexed from side to side at its base.

Inside a shark

Sharks, skates, and rays make up a distinct group of fish called chondrichthyes, or cartilaginous fish. Their skeleton is made not of bone, but of the slightly flexible rubbery cartilage. There are about 715 species in the group. Apart from the skeletal difference, packaged neatly inside a shark's body are all the usual vertebrate organs which keep it alive. The heart pumps the blood around the body, delivering oxygen and nutrients while taking away carbon dioxide and other wastes. Food passes into the digestive system, which is like a large tube. From the mouth the food goes down the gullet into the stomach, where digestion begins, and then into the intestine where digested food is absorbed. Indigestible wastes collect in the rectum to be passed out of the body. Digested food is further processed in the large liver which also increases the shark's buoyancy. Unlike most bony fish, sharks do not have a swim bladder. Kidneys remove wastes from the blood and regulate its concentration. Large muscles in the body wall keep the shark swimming while the skeleton and skin provide support. The brain coordinates the shark's actions with signals or instructions passed back and forth along the spinal cord.

DANGER BELOW
Sharks have been known to attack people coming down into water, as this Australian parachutist will soon discover.

Paired kidneys regulate waste products to keep concentration of body fluids just above that of sea water, or shark will dehydrate

As in other fish, the segmented swimming muscles contract alternately, sending a wave motion from head to tail

Model of a female spinner shark, showing internal anatomy

Vent between claspers for disposing of body wastes

Clasper (male reproductive organ)

Male shark

Female shark

Cloaca (opening for reproduction, and vent for waste disposal)

MALE OR FEMALE
All male sharks have a pair of claspers which are formed from the inner edge of their pelvic fins. During mating, one of the claspers is rotated forwards and inserted into the female's body opening, or cloaca. Sperm is pumped down a groove in the clasper into the female, so fertilization of her eggs takes place inside her body. This is another feature that distinguishes sharks from bony fish.

Rectal gland (third kidney) passes excess salt out of the body through the vent

Scroll valve in intestine, or gut – other sharks have spiral or ring valves

Left lobe of large liver

Caudal fin

ALL IN THE TAIL
Sharks have a backbone, or vertebral column, which extends into the upper lobe of their tail, or caudal fin. This type of caudal fin is called a heterocercal tail, as opposed to those in most bony fish where the upper lobe does not contain an extension of the vertebral column. Cartilaginous rods and dermal filaments help to strengthen the shark's tail.

Vertebral column

Cartilaginous rod

Dermal filament

BRAIN POWER

Some sharks have brains that are similar in weight to those of birds and mammals, when compared to their overall body weight. The nasal sac, or sensory part of the nose, is close to the front part of the brain.

Nasal sac

Forebrain

Midbrain

Hindbrain

Brain of a lemon shark

Ovary (eggs visible within its wall). When ripe, eggs pass into a tube for fertilization

Gill arch with gill filaments, to absorb oxygen from the water

Cartilage support of gill arch, forming a hoop around the gullet

Jaw-opening muscle pulls jaws forwards so teeth protrude

Nostril

Tongue is rigid, supported by a pad of cartilage

Jaw-closing muscle

Cartilage in floor of gullet

Aorta, with branchial arteries

Heart

Open gill slits

BLOOD CIRCULATION

Blood from the body collects in the first chamber of the shark's heart, then is pumped through the second and third, while the fourth prevents blood flowing back into the heart. The aorta and branchial arteries circulate blood to the gills, where each branchial artery divides into tiny blood vessels in the gill filaments. As seawater passes over the gills, oxygen is picked up and carbon dioxide released.

Cartilage at base of pectoral fin

Cartilage of pectoral girdle supports pectoral fins

Shut gill slits

FOOD PROCESSOR

Food begins its digestion process in the shark's stomach, then passes into the intestine, where the multi-layered scroll valve increases the area for absorbing digested food. A greeny-yellowy fluid, stored in the gall bladder, is released into the gut, where it helps fats to be absorbed. The shark's large liver also aids digestion, processing fats, carbohydrates, and proteins.

Gall bladder

Pectoral fin

Second dorsal fin

First dorsal fin

Stomach's descending limb

OPEN, SHUT

To breathe, water comes in through the shark's mouth, passes over the gills, and out of the gill slits. When the mouth opens, the gill slits shut; when the mouth closes, the gill slits open. Sharks lack the gill cover, or operculum, of bony fish.

Anal fin

Pelvic fin

Rear view of whole body of shark, showing gullet

Stomach's ascending limb

Spleen, producing red blood cells

Pancreas, producing enzymes to help digest food in gut

31

The bare bones

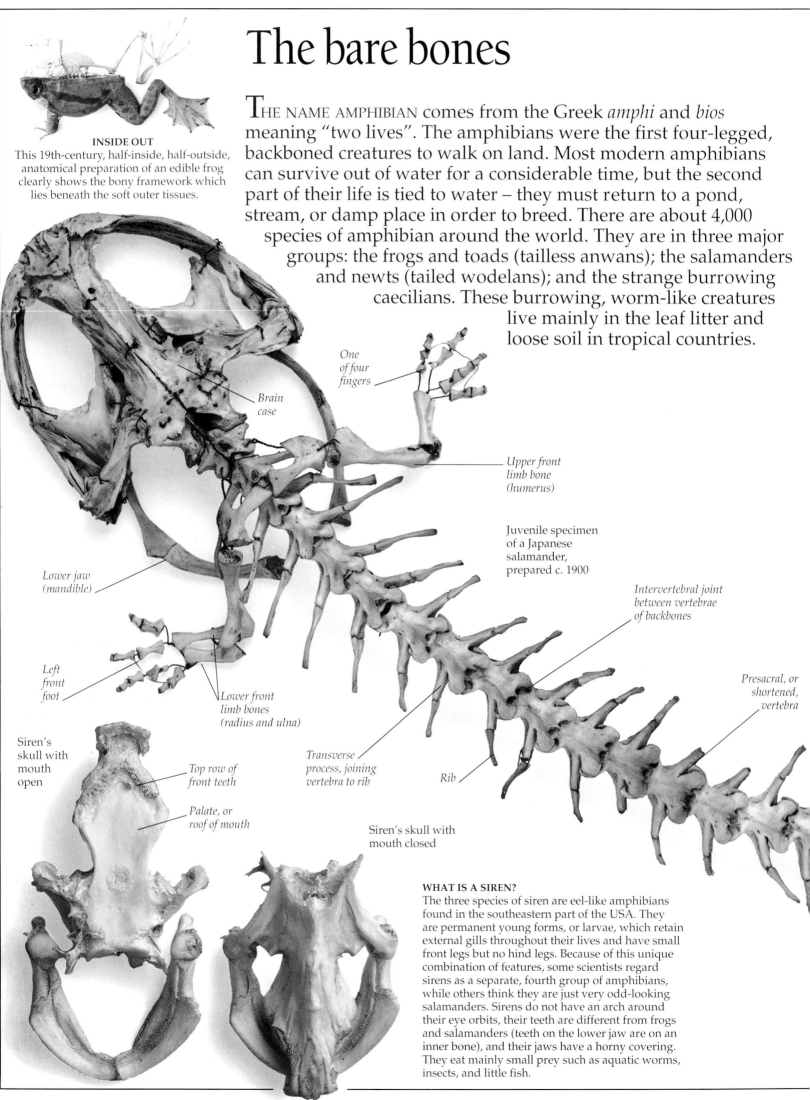

INSIDE OUT
This 19th-century, half-inside, half-outside, anatomical preparation of an edible frog clearly shows the bony framework which lies beneath the soft outer tissues.

THE NAME AMPHIBIAN comes from the Greek *amphi* and *bios* meaning "two lives". The amphibians were the first four-legged, backboned creatures to walk on land. Most modern amphibians can survive out of water for a considerable time, but the second part of their life is tied to water – they must return to a pond, stream, or damp place in order to breed. There are about 4,000 species of amphibian around the world. They are in three major groups: the frogs and toads (tailless anwans); the salamanders and newts (tailed wodelans); and the strange burrowing caecilians. These burrowing, worm-like creatures live mainly in the leaf litter and loose soil in tropical countries.

Brain case

One of four fingers

Upper front limb bone (humerus)

Juvenile specimen of a Japanese salamander, prepared c. 1900

Intervertebral joint between vertebrae of backbones

Lower jaw (mandible)

Left front foot

Lower front limb bones (radius and ulna)

Presacral, or shortened, vertebra

Siren's skull with mouth open

Top row of front teeth

Transverse process, joining vertebra to rib

Rib

Palate, or roof of mouth

Siren's skull with mouth closed

WHAT IS A SIREN?
The three species of siren are eel-like amphibians found in the southeastern part of the USA. They are permanent young forms, or larvae, which retain external gills throughout their lives and have small front legs but no hind legs. Because of this unique combination of features, some scientists regard sirens as a separate, fourth group of amphibians, while others think they are just very odd-looking salamanders. Sirens do not have an arch around their eye orbits, their teeth are different from frogs and salamanders (teeth on the lower jaw are on an inner bone), and their jaws have a horny covering. They eat mainly small prey such as aquatic worms, insects, and little fish.

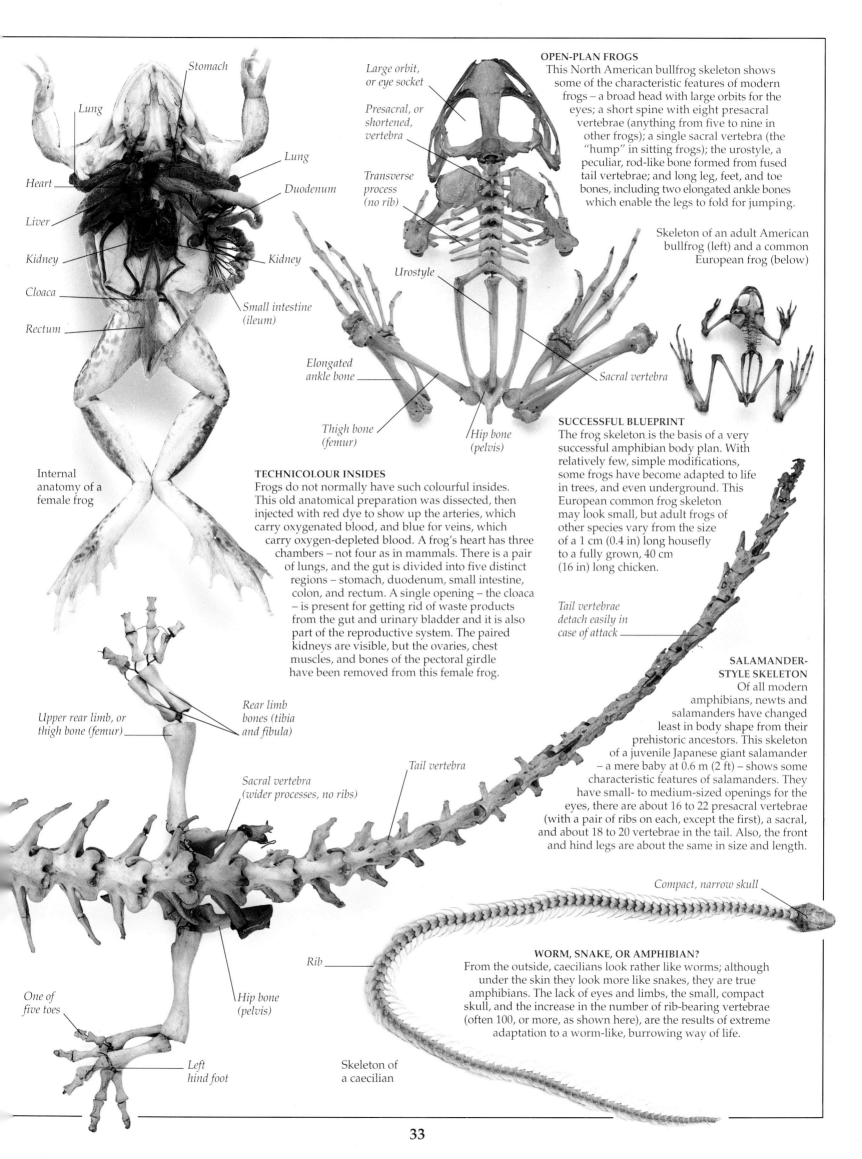

Stomach

Lung

Heart

Liver

Kidney

Cloaca

Rectum

Lung

Duodenum

Kidney

Small intestine (ileum)

Internal anatomy of a female frog

Upper rear limb, or thigh bone (femur)

Rear limb bones (tibia and fibula)

Sacral vertebra (wider processes, no ribs)

Tail vertebra

One of five toes

Hip bone (pelvis)

Left hind foot

Rib

Skeleton of a caecilian

OPEN-PLAN FROGS

This North American bullfrog skeleton shows some of the characteristic features of modern frogs – a broad head with large orbits for the eyes; a short spine with eight presacral vertebrae (anything from five to nine in other frogs); a single sacral vertebra (the "hump" in sitting frogs); the urostyle, a peculiar, rod-like bone formed from fused tail vertebrae; and long leg, feet, and toe bones, including two elongated ankle bones which enable the legs to fold for jumping.

Large orbit, or eye socket

Presacral, or shortened, vertebra

Transverse process (no rib)

Urostyle

Elongated ankle bone

Thigh bone (femur)

Hip bone (pelvis)

Sacral vertebra

Skeleton of an adult American bullfrog (left) and a common European frog (below)

TECHNICOLOUR INSIDES

Frogs do not normally have such colourful insides. This old anatomical preparation was dissected, then injected with red dye to show up the arteries, which carry oxygenated blood, and blue for veins, which carry oxygen-depleted blood. A frog's heart has three chambers – not four as in mammals. There is a pair of lungs, and the gut is divided into five distinct regions – stomach, duodenum, small intestine, colon, and rectum. A single opening – the cloaca – is present for getting rid of waste products from the gut and urinary bladder and it is also part of the reproductive system. The paired kidneys are visible, but the ovaries, chest muscles, and bones of the pectoral girdle have been removed from this female frog.

SUCCESSFUL BLUEPRINT

The frog skeleton is the basis of a very successful amphibian body plan. With relatively few, simple modifications, some frogs have become adapted to life in trees, and even underground. This European common frog skeleton may look small, but adult frogs of other species vary from the size of a 1 cm (0.4 in) long housefly to a fully grown, 40 cm (16 in) long chicken.

Tail vertebrae detach easily in case of attack

SALAMANDER-STYLE SKELETON

Of all modern amphibians, newts and salamanders have changed least in body shape from their prehistoric ancestors. This skeleton of a juvenile Japanese giant salamander – a mere baby at 0.6 m (2 ft) – shows some characteristic features of salamanders. They have small- to medium-sized openings for the eyes, there are about 16 to 22 presacral vertebrae (with a pair of ribs on each, except the first), a sacral, and about 18 to 20 vertebrae in the tail. Also, the front and hind legs are about the same in size and length.

Compact, narrow skull

WORM, SNAKE, OR AMPHIBIAN?

From the outside, caecilians look rather like worms; although under the skin they look more like snakes, they are true amphibians. The lack of eyes and limbs, the small, compact skull, and the increase in the number of rib-bearing vertebrae (often 100, or more, as shown here), are the results of extreme adaptation to a worm-like, burrowing way of life.

Legs or legless?

Reptiles have the same basic skeleton and main internal organs as other four-limbed (quadruped) vertebrates such as amphibians, birds, and mammals. But in many reptiles, bone growth does not stop at maturity, which means that some reptiles keep growing throughout their lives. If a reptile survives the everyday dangers of life, it may eventually become giant-sized. This is particularly true of pythons, crocodiles, and giant tortoises. Snakes are unusual in that they have lost almost all traces of their limbs during evolution to become the main group of legless vertebrates.

Tail vertebrae

Intestine

Bood vessel

Inside a lizard

Trunk vertebrae

Chameleon skeleton

Skull

Ribs

CHAMELEON
Many lizards have highly specialized skeletons. The chameleon, for example, is adapted for life in trees and bushes. The body is narrow and deep, providing greater stability when the animal's weight is centred over a narrow twig or branch. The fingers and toes are designed for grasping, with three toes on the outside and two on the inside of the foot, and the other way round on the hand. The tail is prehensile, which means it can grasp and hold like a fifth limb.

CAIMAN
The caiman is a type of crocodile from South America. Its skull is long, with the eye sockets and nostrils set high, so that the caiman can float with just its nose and eyes above the water. Its body is long as well, with two pairs of rather short legs, and five toes on the front feet and four on the back feet. The toes on all the feet are partly webbed. The upper jaw of the caiman, as with all other members of the crocodile family, is almost solid bone.

Skull

Caiman skeleton

Neck vertebrae

Ribs

Tail vertebrae

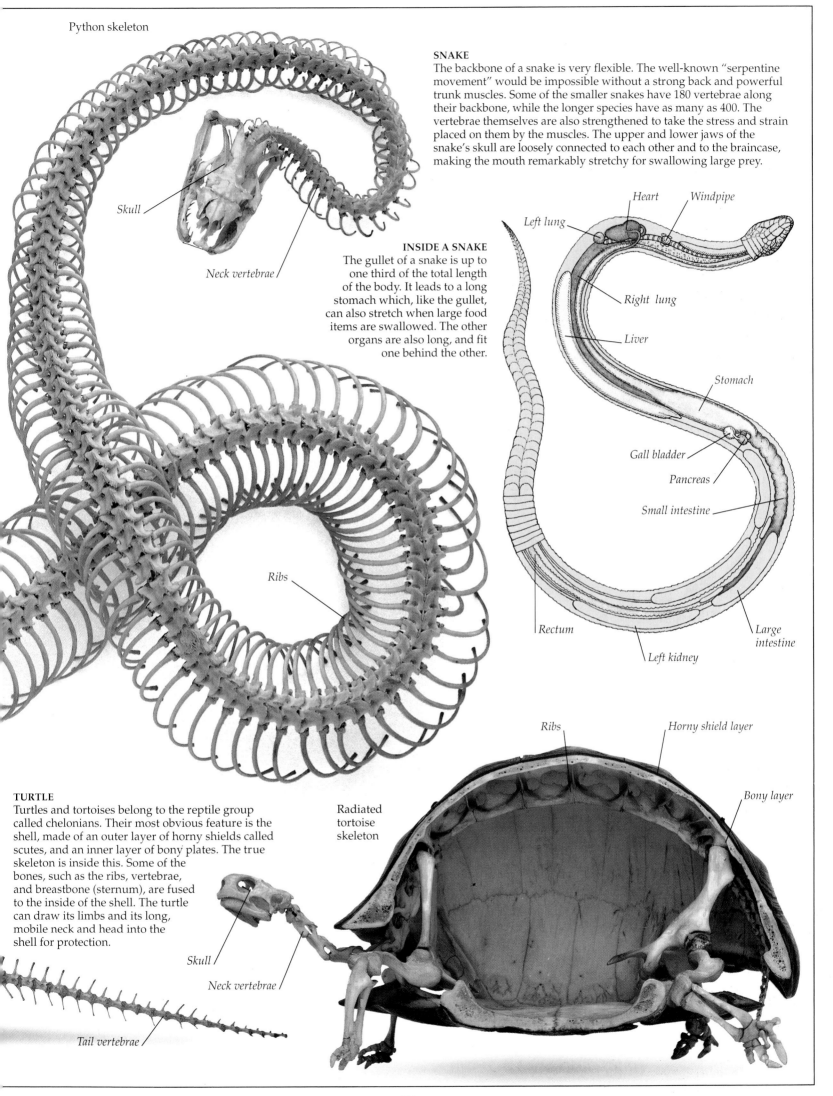

Python skeleton

Skull

Neck vertebrae

Ribs

SNAKE
The backbone of a snake is very flexible. The well-known "serpentine movement" would be impossible without a strong back and powerful trunk muscles. Some of the smaller snakes have 180 vertebrae along their backbone, while the longer species have as many as 400. The vertebrae themselves are also strengthened to take the stress and strain placed on them by the muscles. The upper and lower jaws of the snake's skull are loosely connected to each other and to the braincase, making the mouth remarkably stretchy for swallowing large prey.

INSIDE A SNAKE
The gullet of a snake is up to one third of the total length of the body. It leads to a long stomach which, like the gullet, can also stretch when large food items are swallowed. The other organs are also long, and fit one behind the other.

Heart

Windpipe

Left lung

Right lung

Liver

Stomach

Gall bladder

Pancreas

Small intestine

Large intestine

Rectum

Left kidney

Ribs

Horny shield layer

Bony layer

TURTLE
Turtles and tortoises belong to the reptile group called chelonians. Their most obvious feature is the shell, made of an outer layer of horny shields called scutes, and an inner layer of bony plates. The true skeleton is inside this. Some of the bones, such as the ribs, vertebrae, and breastbone (sternum), are fused to the inside of the shell. The turtle can draw its limbs and its long, mobile neck and head into the shell for protection.

Radiated tortoise skeleton

Skull

Neck vertebrae

Tail vertebrae

Taking to the air

*Archaeopteryx –
the primaeval bird*

IN THE LONG HISTORY OF EVOLUTION, birds were not the first creatures to fly. That achievement belongs to insects. Neither were they the first large flying animals. This honour belongs to the winged reptiles called pterosaurs, which appeared during the Age of Dinosaurs, around 200 million years ago. But today, birds are the dominant form of life in the air. There are about 9,000 species of birds, and they occupy virtually every habitat on Earth, from the terns, geese, and albatrosses soaring near the frozen poles, to the parrots and hummingbirds of steamy tropical forests. Penguins, divers, and similar seabirds are completely at home even in the water of the oceans. The earliest known bird is preserved as one of the world's most famous fossils, called *Archaeopteryx*, or ancient wing. Although this creature lived over 150 million years ago, when the pterosaurs were still in their heyday, the fossils show that this crow-sized animal was thickly feathered. And it is the possession of feathers that makes a bird a bird.

THE FIRST LINK
The first *Archaeopteryx* fossil was found in Germany in 1861, in an area which was once flooded by sea. When the animal died, its body was covered by fine silt which preserved not only the outlines of bones, but also those of feathers. Over millions of years, this compressed silt gradually became limestone, and when it was quarried, the stone yielded up the fossils. In this specimen, the bird-like wings and legs are clearly visible, as are the reptilian teeth and tail. It is likely that *Archaeopteryx* evolved from small dinosaurs that ran upright instead of walking on all fours. Seven *Archaeopteryx* fossils have been found, all from the same area in Bavaria.

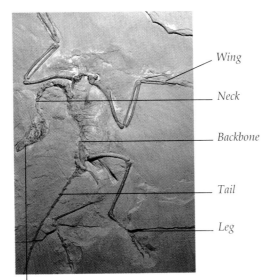

Wing

Neck

Backbone

Tail

Leg

Head

STAYING BALANCED
Compared to many animals, birds are compact creatures. A bird's legs, wings, and neck are all lightweight structures. The heavy parts, particularly the wing and leg muscles, are packed closely around the ribcage and backbone. This allows a bird to stay balanced both on the wing and on the ground.

Front view of a crow's skeleton

Skull

Neck

Backbone

Wishbone

Coracoid bone

Ribcage

Breastbone

Leg bones

EVOLUTIONARY EXPERIMENT
Although fossils show that pterosaurs were highly successful in their time, they died out with the dinosaurs 65 million years ago. They were not ancestors of modern birds.

AS DEAD AS THE DODO
The dodo was a flightless bird of Madagascar and neighbouring islands in the Indian Ocean, and was driven to extinction by humans in the late 17th century. When Lewis Carroll described the encounter between the dodo and Alice in his book *Through the Looking Glass*, the species was already "as dead as a dodo". Flying birds have also suffered from human hunting and persecution. The last passenger pigeon died in 1914, whereas 100 years earlier, the species formed flocks in North America over a *billion* strong.

Eye socket

Nostril

Cranium made of fused bones

Upper maxilla of beak

Ear

Lower mandible of beak

Although they differ in size, flying birds like the crow have a very similar overall shape. This is because they all need to be streamlined, and cannot afford structures that would mean carrying extra weight.

THE BIRD SKELETON

The evolution of powered flight has left birds with skeletons that are quite unlike those of other animals. The most obvious feature in a flying bird like the crow is its huge keel, the projection from the breastbone which anchors the muscles of the wings. Birds do not have teeth, and neither do they have true tails; the tail feathers are attached to a bony stump called the pygostyle. The forelimbs are completely adapted for use in flight, while the toothless jaws have evolved into a lightweight but very strong break which the bird can use for feeding and delicate tasks such as preening.

Coracoid bone

Backbone, made up of small bones called vertebrae, can bend where the vertebrae are linked by flexible joints, but is rigid where they are fused together

Humerus, an elongated wing bone, corresponding to the human upper arm bone

Radius, a wing bone, corresponding to one of the human forearm bones

Back view of a crow's skeleton

Skull

Neck

Wishbone, made up of two joined collarbones, helps to keep the wing joint in position as the wing muscles pull downwards

Ulna, a wing bone, corresponding to the second human forearm bone

Backbone

Humerus

Radius

Keel, which anchors the wing muscles of flying birds

Hip girdle or pelvis provides support for the legs, and large anchoring surfaces for the leg muscles

Metacarpus, corresponding to the human wrist bone

Ulna

Knee joint (hidden by feathers in the living bird)

Lower leg bone (tibia)

Pygostyle, bony stump to which tail feathers are attached

Claw (in living bird, covered in horny sheath)

Pelvis

Ankle or false knee – although it may look as if the knee bends back to front, this is actually the bird's ankle, not its knee

Pygostyle

Three forward-facing toes

Tarsus

Hind toe

Wing power

THREE GROUPS OF ANIMALS – insects, bats, and birds – are capable of powered flight. Of these, birds are by far the largest, fastest, and most powerful fliers. The secret of their success lies in the design of their wings. A bird's wing is light, strong, and flexible. It is also slightly curved like an aircraft wing, producing an aerofoil profile which literally pulls the bird upwards as it flaps through the air. Although wing size and shape vary according to each bird's lifestyle, they all share the same basic pattern, shown here in the wing of an owl.

OVER THE LIMIT
A bird's wings can bear its weight, plus light luggage such as food and nesting materials. Heavier loads, like human passengers, are strictly out of the question.

FLIGHT OF FANCY
Legend describes how Icarus flew from Crete to Greece. He climbed too near to the Sun and the wax that held his feathers melted. But birds flying at high altitude have to cope with quite different and much more real problems – thin air, scarce oxygen, and intense cold.

ALULA
This group of feathers, also called the bastard wing, is held open in slow flight to prevent stalling.

MECHANICAL MIMICRY
A brilliant artist, inventor, and anatomist, Leonardo da Vinci drew on his knowledge of bird wings to design machines that would imitate their flight. He replaced bones with wood, tendons with ropes, and feathers with sailcloth. As far as is known, none of these devices ever got beyond his drawing board. They would have been far too heavy to fly.

FLAPPING FAILURES
The heroic birdmen of bygone days did not realize that flapping flight would always be beyond the power of human muscles. True human-powered flight has only been achieved through the later invention of the propeller, and using leg muscles, not arms.

PRIMARY FLIGHT FEATHERS
The primaries make the power for flight as the bird brings its wings downwards. The outermost primaries can be used for steering, like the flaps on a plane's wing.

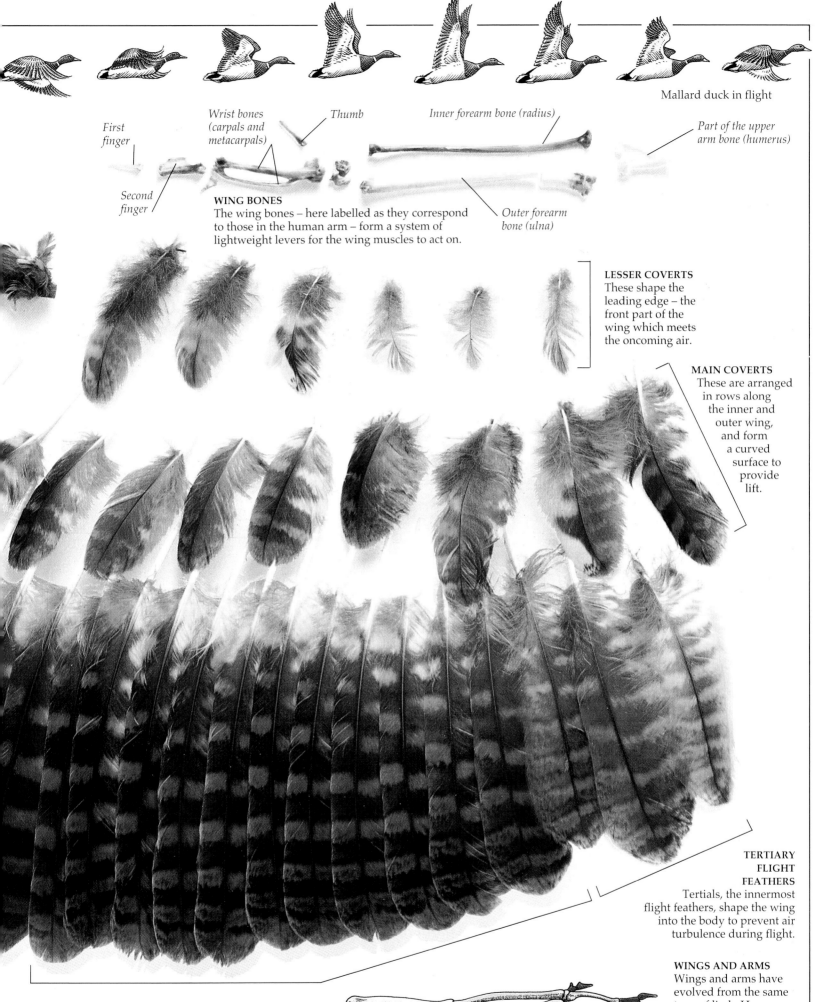

Mallard duck in flight

First finger

Second finger

Wrist bones (carpals and metacarpals)

Thumb

Inner forearm bone (radius)

Part of the upper arm bone (humerus)

WING BONES
The wing bones – here labelled as they correspond to those in the human arm – form a system of lightweight levers for the wing muscles to act on.

Outer forearm bone (ulna)

LESSER COVERTS
These shape the leading edge – the front part of the wing which meets the oncoming air.

MAIN COVERTS
These are arranged in rows along the inner and outer wing, and form a curved surface to provide lift.

TERTIARY FLIGHT FEATHERS
Tertials, the innermost flight feathers, shape the wing into the body to prevent air turbulence during flight.

SECONDARY FLIGHT FEATHERS
On the inner wing, the secondaries form the aerofoil curve that provides lift.

Bones of the bird's wing

Bones of the human arm

WINGS AND ARMS
Wings and arms have evolved from the same type of limb. However, the wing has only three digits, and some of the wrist bones are fused together. Here, the corresponding bones are the same colour.

The feather phenomenon

FEATHERS ARE THE UNIQUE evolutionary innovation that separates birds from all other animals. The plumage of a hummingbird may number less than 1,000 feathers, while a large bird like a swan may have over 25,000, with nearly four-fifths of these covering the head and neck alone. Like hair, claws, and horns, feathers are made from a protein called keratin, which gives feathers their great strength and flexibility. But for all their intricate structure, fully grown feathers are quite dead. As each feather develops, it divides to form a complex mesh of interlocking filaments. Once this has happened, its blood supply is cut off. The feathers then serve their time, unless lost by accident, and are shed during moulting when they are worn out.

BREAKABLE PLUMAGE
The Central American motmot changes the shape of its tail feathers during preening. When it pecks at a tail feather, the feather's barbs break off to leave a bare shaft ending in a spoon-shaped tip. Quite why it does this has not yet been discovered.

Feather sheaths

Emerging feather tufts

Growing feathers within sheaths

HOW FEATHERS GROW
Feathers start their growth as fleshy lumps inside tubes known as feather sheaths. The tip of a feather gradually begins to emerge from the growing sheath, unrolling and splitting apart to form a flat blade. Eventually the feather sheath falls away, leaving the fully formed feather.

FEATHER SHAFT
The hollow shaft contains the dried remains of the fleshy pulp.

Hollow interior

Pulp from interior of shaft

Fully grown feathers after the protective sheaths have fallen away

Quill tip embedded in skin and attached to muscles

WEARING FEATHERS
Feathers have long been used by people for adornment and for more practical purposes. Head-dresses and quill pens both made use of flight feathers. The down feathers of ducks and geese are still collected for bedding, while the brilliantly coloured plumes of some tropical birds find their way into objects such as fishing flies.

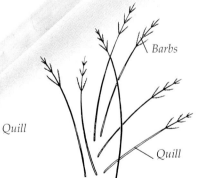

Barbs

Quill

Quill

FILOPLUMES
These hair-like growths are found between the feathers on a bird's body. They help the bird to detect how its feathers are lying.

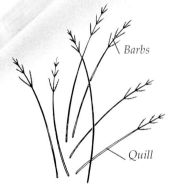

Aftershaft, second shaft from a single quill

SPLIT FEATHERS
Some feathers are split to form two different halves attached to the same shaft. This enables a single feather to perform two different functions.

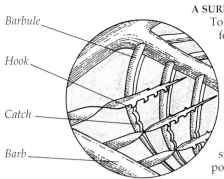

Barbule

Hook

Catch

Barb

A SURFACE FOR FLIGHT
To work effectively, a flight feather has to form a single continuous surface, which air must flow over, not through. This surface is produced by thousands of barbules. These lie on either side of each barb and lock together as hooks and catches. If barbule hooks become disengaged, a bird simply preens them back into position with its beak.

Feather tip

Notch for reducing turbulence

Outer vane (windward edge of feather)

Rachis or shaft

Downward edge

Upcurved edge

Inner vane (leeward or trailing edge of feather)

Parallel barbs locked together to form a smooth surface

Further magnification of macaw feather

Scarlet macaw flight feather magnified to show barbs and barbules

FEATHERS WITHIN FEATHERS
Under high magnification, barbs and barbules look almost like miniature feathers. On flight feathers like this, the barbs are closely packed, while the barbules are short and numerous. By contrast, the barbs on down feathers are less numerous and much longer. Down feathers are soft and fluffy, and are mainly for insulation. Some down feathers have no barbules at all.

Feather care

Feathers receive a tremendous battering during daily use, and in addition, they easily become dirty and infested with parasites such as feather lice. Most feathers are shed every year during moulting, but nevertheless, birds have to spend much of their time ensuring that their plumage stays in an airworthy condition. They do this by preening, using the beak like a comb to draw together their feathers' barbs and barbules. There are also special methods of feather care, such as oiling, powdering, and bathing, both in water and in dust.

POWDERED PLUMAGE
Egrets, herons, and some other birds have special feathers which disintegrate to form a powder. This "powder down" is used to keep the plumage in good condition. Unlike other feathers, powder down feathers never stop growing.

DUST BATHS
Dust is both absorbent and abrasive. Bathing in dust cleans a bird's plumage by scouring dirt from the feathers.

ANTING JAYS
Jays sometimes encourage ants to swarm over their feathers. Poisonous formic acid is produced by the ants, and may dislodge parasites living in the jay's plumage or on its skin.

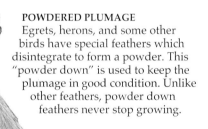

Mammal skeletons

Mammals SUCH AS dogs, cats, monkeys, and ourselves all have the same general skeleton design. This is similar in overall structure to the skeletons of birds, reptiles, and amphibians. As in these other vertebrates, the bones of the skeleton provide a supporting framework, surfaces for muscle anchorage, and protection. The spine is the main support for the body, flexible at its joints, yet able to be held rigid by the body muscles. The skull houses and protects the brain and the delicate organs of sight, hearing, smell, and taste. The ribs form a protective cage around the heart and lungs. Each of the four limbs is basically the same: It has one long upper bone, two long lower bones, several smaller bones (wrist or ankle) and five digits (fingers or toes). Mammal skeletons come in different shapes and sizes, adapted to their surroundings and way of life.

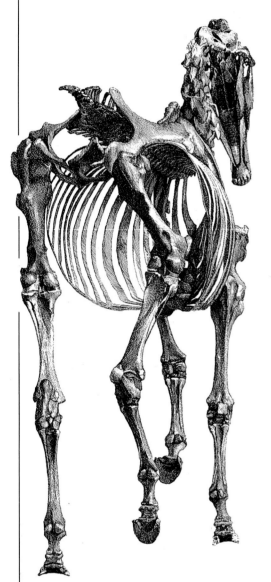

Many of the larger mammals are now extinct, like this mammoth

INSIDE KNOWLEDGE
George Stubbs, the 18th-century animal painter, spent two years studying horse anatomy. This is one of his drawings of a horse skeleton, done in 1766.

Spine

Shoulder blade (scapula)

Hip bone

Badger skeleton

Rib cage

Tail vertebrae

Hind limbs are at an angle giving badger its distinctive posture

BADGER'S DESIGN FOR DIGGING
The squat, powerfully built badger is not known for its fleetness of foot. Its thick-boned limbs, strong feet, and long claws are designed for digging tunnels and scratching into the earth for small creatures to eat. Its teeth are those of a meat eater, although the badger eats berries and other plant food too.

Upper arm bone (humerus)

Inner forearm bone (radius)

Outer forearm bone (ulna)

Toes bear claws for digging up soil

Lower leg bones (tibia and fibula)

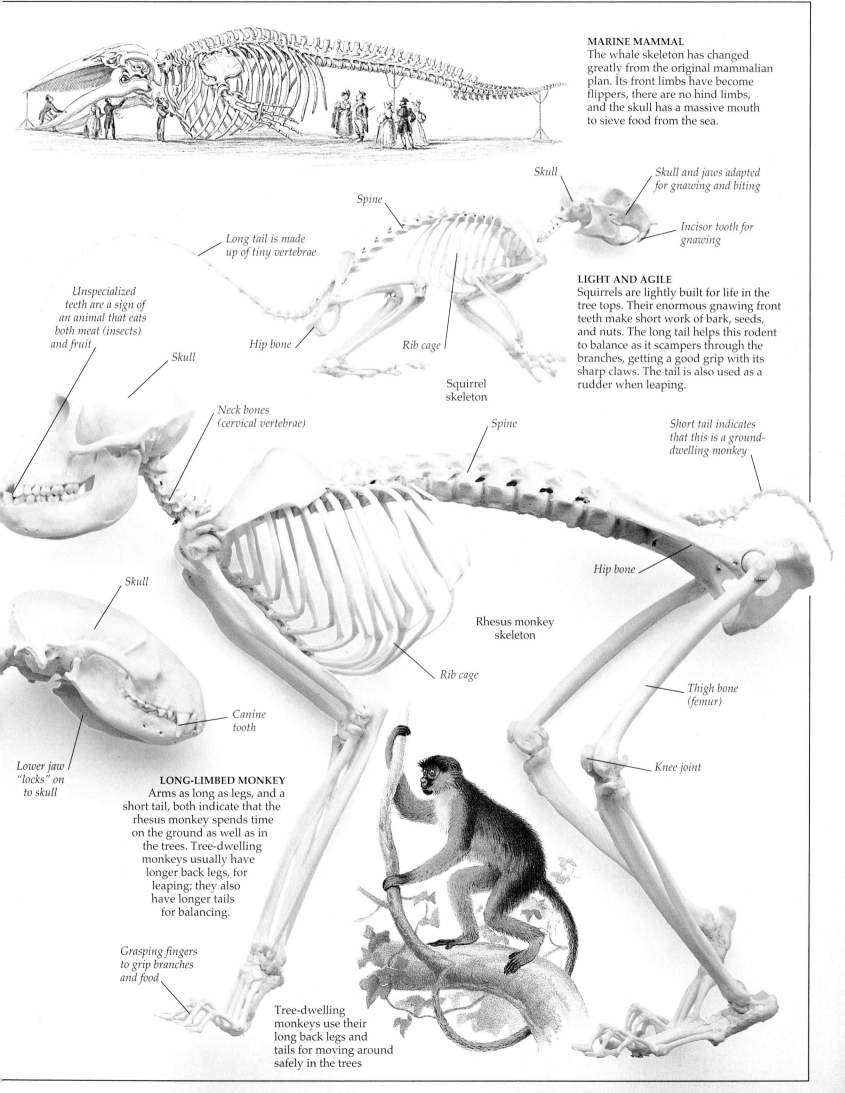

MARINE MAMMAL
The whale skeleton has changed greatly from the original mammalian plan. Its front limbs have become flippers, there are no hind limbs, and the skull has a massive mouth to sieve food from the sea.

Skull

Skull and jaws adapted for gnawing and biting

Spine

Incisor tooth for gnawing

Long tail is made up of tiny vertebrae

LIGHT AND AGILE
Squirrels are lightly built for life in the tree tops. Their enormous gnawing front teeth make short work of bark, seeds, and nuts. The long tail helps this rodent to balance as it scampers through the branches, getting a good grip with its sharp claws. The tail is also used as a rudder when leaping.

Hip bone

Rib cage

Squirrel skeleton

Unspecialized teeth are a sign of an animal that eats both meat (insects) and fruit

Skull

Neck bones (cervical vertebrae)

Spine

Short tail indicates that this is a ground-dwelling monkey

Hip bone

Rhesus monkey skeleton

Skull

Rib cage

Thigh bone (femur)

Canine tooth

Knee joint

Lower jaw "locks" on to skull

LONG-LIMBED MONKEY
Arms as long as legs, and a short tail, both indicate that the rhesus monkey spends time on the ground as well as in the trees. Tree-dwelling monkeys usually have longer back legs, for leaping; they also have longer tails for balancing.

Grasping fingers to grip branches and food

Tree-dwelling monkeys use their long back legs and tails for moving around safely in the trees

Largest on land

The ELEPHANT is the largest living land mammal. During evolution, its skeleton has greatly altered from the usual mammal design for two main reasons. One is to cope with the great weight of huge grinding cheek teeth and elongated tusk teeth, making the skull particularly massive. The other is to support the enormous bulk of such a huge body. The elephant has all the usual internal parts of any mammal such as muscles, nerves, and internal organs including a heart, lungs, and intestines. But these have become proportionally gigantic – the heart alone is the weight of a 9-year-old child. When an elephant stands at rest, the bones in each leg stack one above the other to form a sturdy pillar. This is how an elephant can relax, and even fall asleep while standing up – and not fall over. There are slight differences between the two species of elephants, African and Asian, as shown here.

Tusk sockets

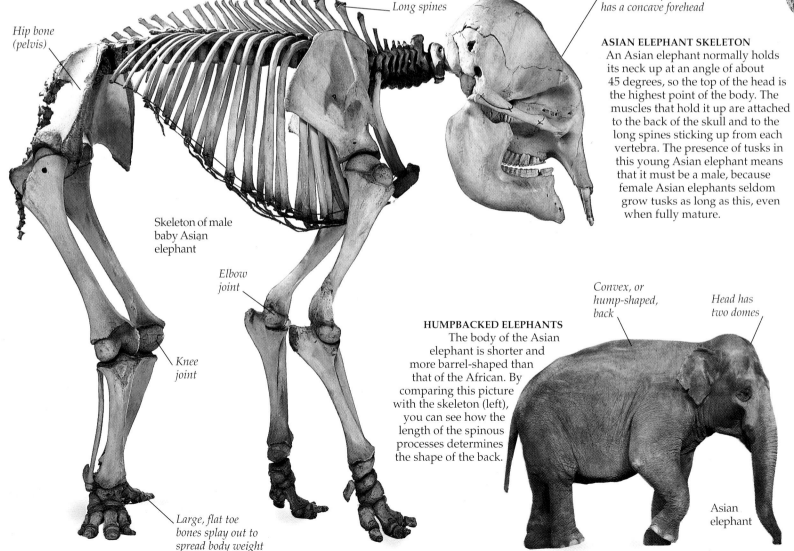

Long spines

*Hip bone
(pelvis)*

*An Asian elephant
has a concave forehead*

ASIAN ELEPHANT SKELETON
An Asian elephant normally holds its neck up at an angle of about 45 degrees, so the top of the head is the highest point of the body. The muscles that hold it up are attached to the back of the skull and to the long spines sticking up from each vertebra. The presence of tusks in this young Asian elephant means that it must be a male, because female Asian elephants seldom grow tusks as long as this, even when fully mature.

Skeleton of male
baby Asian
elephant

*Elbow
joint*

*Knee
joint*

HUMPBACKED ELEPHANTS
The body of the Asian elephant is shorter and more barrel-shaped than that of the African. By comparing this picture with the skeleton (left), you can see how the length of the spinous processes determines the shape of the back.

*Convex, or
hump-shaped,
back*

*Head has
two domes*

*Large, flat toe
bones splay out to
spread body weight*

Asian
elephant

BUILT LIKE BRIDGES
Elephants, stone bridges, and arches all work on the same mechanical principle, and so have a similar design. They all share the weight of their load between their supports. With the load-bearing part curving upwards in the middle, they can carry a far greater load.

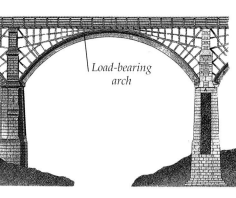

Load-bearing arch

AIR HEADS
Although elephants have big brains (up to four times the size of a human brain), the brain does not fill the whole skull, as can be seen in this African elephant skull which has been sawn in half. Above the brain case the bone is not solid but forms a honeycomb of hollow cavities that make it lighter than it looks.

Air cavities (diploe)

Brain case

Upper grinding tooth – lower jaw is not shown

The spinous processes determine the shape of the elephant's back

Skeleton of female adult African elephant

AFRICAN ELEPHANT SKELETON
African elephants usually hold their neck horizontally, so the highest point of the body is formed by the long spines on the vertebrae between the shoulder blades. The skull of a male African elephant has a smooth, rounded forehead, whereas that of a female, like the one pictured here, has an angular bump on top.

TYPICAL MAMMALS
This cat skeleton is shown on the same scale as the elephant skeleton. It has the same individual bones, but these are of the more typical mammalian design. The limb bones are long and slim, the backbone is lithe and flexible, and the skull is proportionally small.

Massive leg bones support the elephant's weight

This adult elephant skeleton is about 11 times taller than this adult cat skeleton

The highest part of the body is between the shoulder blades

The African elephant's back is concave

African elephant

SWAY-BACKED ELEPHANTS
African elephants have longer legs and a more streamlined appearance than Asian elephants. Compare this photograph with the skeleton (above) to see how the short spinous processes in the middle of the back make the elephant appear to have a concave back.

Coats and claws

THE NATURAL WORLD is full of hairy creatures, from "woolly bear" caterpillars to tarantula spiders. But mammals are the only animals with true fur. Fur is made from the substance keratin, which is the same material that makes up the outer layer of mammalian skin, as well as your fingernails and toenails. Fur is very versatile. It can be thick or thin, long or short, according to the mammal's habitat and needs. It keeps its owner warm and protected, and its patterning acts as camouflage, or as a breeding or warning signal.

CURLY AND STRAIGHT
This domestic cat has been bred for its unusual curly fur. The fur of most mammals is much straighter. This is so that water runs off it more easily, and it is less likely to trap dirt and pests. But the "fur" on humans – the hair on our heads – can be straight, wavy, or curly.

Close-up fur

Close up, mammals reveal the delicate shading and patterning on their fur. This young lioness still has the spotty coloration from her time as a young cub, although the spots are gradually fading.

SPOT ME
The colours and patterns of some mammals, such as this leopard, have evolved to give camouflage in the animal's natural habitat. They may stand out in a zoo in broad daylight, but in the light conditions at dusk, when the leopard is normally active, its spotted coat merges in with the wooded grasslands.

FUR COATS
All the colours and patterns in mammal fur are produced by melanin – a pigment, or colouring substance. It exists as tiny dark brown particles inside the microscopic cells that make up skin and hair. The colouring effect comes from the amount of melanin in each hair, and its precise position in the hair shaft. Here are the coats of six cats, showing their intricate and characteristic markings.

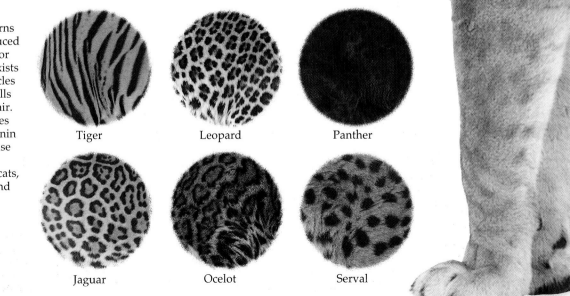

Tiger

Leopard

Panther

Jaguar

Ocelot

Serval

Cat claws

A cat can unsheath its claws by a muscle in each leg and foot. As the muscle contracts, it pulls the claw down and forwards. Normally the muscle is relaxed, and the claw retracted.

Relaxed, with claw withdrawn into toe

Muscle and ligament tightened to expose claw

PAINFUL PETS
Many mammals rub and sharpen their claws, as a natural habit to keep them smooth and in working order. With pets, this can lead to painful problems!

ADJUSTABLE DUVET
A tiny muscle at the base of each hair, embedded in the skin, can tighten to make the hair stand up straight, or relax to let it lie flat. Fluffed up fur traps more air between the hairs, to improve heat-retaining abilities. It may also stand on end so the owner looks bigger and fiercer when confronting danger. These cats are warm and comfortable, so their fur lies fairly flat.

HOOVES
Keratin is light, strong, and durable, and also makes the hooves of the hoofed mammals, or ungulates. Horses have only one large toe in each foot and stand on the toe tip. In human terms, this zebra runs on the nail of its middle fingers and toes.

CLAWS
Keratin makes up the claws of various mammals. Cat claws can be withdrawn into the flesh and muscles of the toes to keep them sharp (see top). The claws of this lioness are almost hidden in the fleshy folds and fur of her toes. The leathery pads on her soles are yet another form of the ever-useful keratin. They give good grip and are very hard-wearing, and also allow silent stalking.

HIDDEN CURVES
Fluffy fur gives a false impression of the real shape and curves of a mammal's body. With its fur and skin gone, and the outer layer of muscles exposed, this cat looks strangely thin, long-necked, and small-headed.

BIG HUNTER
The great white shark is a top carnivore (meat eater). It does little except feed and breed. With an ultra-sharp sense of smell, a mouth full of triangular-bladed teeth, and a powerful swishing tail, the shark is a complete hunting machine.

CHAPTER 2

HUNTING & FEEDING

FOOD IS THE FUEL and raw material for life. Every animal must eat to live, and there are almost as many different foods, and ways of obtaining them, as there are different kinds of hungry animal.

SMALL HUNTERS
Piranhas play the role of freshwater mini-sharks. They have razor-sharp teeth and gather around a wounded animal and tear flesh from the body. What piranhas lack in size, they make up for in numbers. The ecological balance of nature allows smaller predators to be more numerous, since the same amount of food can fuel one large body or several smaller ones.

A question of taste

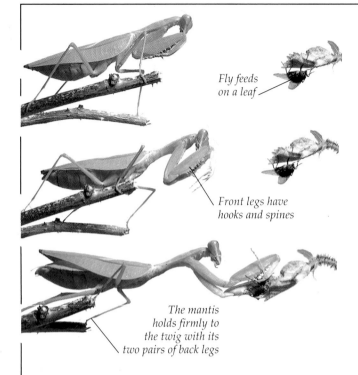

Fly feeds
on a leaf

Front legs have
hooks and spines

The mantis
holds firmly to
the twig with its
two pairs of back legs

W~E OFTEN HEAR~ that one animal is a carnivore, or fresh-meat eater, while another is a herbivore, or fresh-plant eater. It is true that, given the choice, animals tend to stick to creatures or plants for their main food, but a very hungry animal will eat almost anything. For example, a wolf is normally a carnivore, chasing and killing caribou and other victims. But it will also rip rotting meat from a carcass, which is called scavenging. It also takes the occasional snack of berries or fruits, or perhaps insects.

FUSSY FLY-EATER
The praying mantis is an insectivore – its diet is made up mostly of insects. It stays motionless on a twig, while its eyes swivel to watch a fly. When the fly is within range, the mantis grabs it with its front legs in a flash. The mantis then uses its mouthparts to scoop out all the soft flesh and fluids, leaving the tough, indigestible wings and legs.

The toucan's bill is
hollow and light

The serrated edges of
the beak allow the
toucan to bite off
chunks of fruit

A PASSION FOR FRUITS
The toucan's huge beak looks like a fearsome weapon for pecking prey to death. But it is really a very light, hollow, delicate tool for picking fruit. This bird is a frugivore, or fruit eater, and a gramnivore, or seed eater. It adores passionfruits, berries, and other soft fruits, as well as seeds. The beak is extraordinarily large because it has another function, too. Each toucan's beak is a slightly different size, shape, and colour. So it is a personal "flag" allowing individual toucans to recognize each other across forest clearings.

The outside of the beak is made
of hard keratin – the same
material as your fingernails

Toucans have sharp eyesight for seeing food, friends, and enemies in the tropical woodlands where they live

A FONDNESS FOR FISH
The caiman is a close relative of crocodiles and alligators, and comes from South America. It is a true carnivore – it eats fresh meat. The meat may be frogs or small fish, or mammals such as the pig-sized peccary.

Strong sharp teeth for tearing meat

Hunters' weapons

DURING MILLIONS of years of evolution, almost every part of the body of various hunting animals has become adapted to the pursuit and capture of prey. In many creatures, from cats and dogs to crocodiles and dinosaurs, the teeth and perhaps claws are the primary weapons. All spiders and centipedes, and some snakes, have combined physical and chemical weapons – poison-injecting fangs. In carnivorous insects such as mantises, the front legs help to grasp and subdue victims. Some bats catch their airborne prey in a "scoop" formed by the legs and tail membrane. Even apparently slow, simple, ill-equipped animals can be successful predators. The starfish has muscular arms to prise open its prey of mussels and other shellfish.

CLOSE-QUARTER WEAPONS
These curved claws, as big as your hand, are over 100 million years old. They are fossilized dinosaur remains. The left one is a foot claw from *Albertosaurus*, a fearsome meat-eater resembling *Tyrannosaurus*. The right one is a hand claw from *Chirostenotes*, a small predatory dinosaur.

DETECTION
Most bats use a sound radar system called echolocation. They emit high-pitched sounds and, from the pattern of returning echoes, work out the shape and position of nearby objects. This horseshoe bat has detected an oak beauty moth (right).

Between the scales, the snake's skin is blue

RE-ORIENTATION

The bat changes its direction and orientates itself towards its quarry. It keeps sending out its ultrasonic pulses, through the specially designed nose-leaf or "horseshoe". As it gains a better fix on the prey, the bat adjusts its own flight path to intercept.

The arm bones in the wing alter the wing shape for acrobatic manoeuvres

Ears swivel to pick up echoes

FINAL APPROACH

As the bat closes in, it may be able to see the moth in the gloom. But its eyes are small and its line of sight is partially obscured by the nose-leaf. Vision plays little part in the horseshoe bat's hunting because its echolocation is so detailed and efficient.

Great oak beauty

CAPTURE

This moth is an example of larger prey which the horseshoe bat will catch and then take back to its roost to eat. Smaller items, like gnats, are swallowed at once on the wing. The horseshoe usually grabs its prey in its jaws. Some bats scoop up their prey with the tail, while others grab it with the long claws on their feet.

Front part of body sticks out stock still, like an old branch in the gloom

Eyes are very sensitive to movement but not to stationary objects

LEGLESS PREDATOR

The red-tailed racer is, like all snakes, a stealthy hunter. It can move very fast, and sometimes pursues prey such as lizards or small mammals. But it usually catches its prey by staying still. Its tongue flicks out to catch the scent of an approaching meal. The racer may hang around a bat roost, pretending to be part of a branch or boulder. When a bat flies within reach, the snake grabs it in its wide-gaping mouth, then crushes it to death with its muscular body. Snakes have no limbs with which to tear up their victim, and their teeth are designed only for grabbing. So the snake opens its mouth wide, unhinges its jaws, and swallows the prey whole.

Tongue gathers scents in the air and passes them to a smell organ, called the Jacobson's organ, in the roof of the mouth

Tentacles and stings

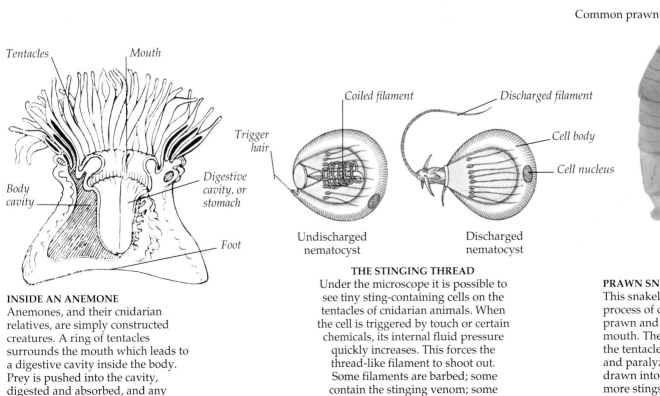

THE CNIDARIAN, or coelenterate, animals include the jellyfish, sea anemones, and corals. There are about 9,400 species and the vast majority live in the sea. They are relatively simple creatures which lack a brain and sophisticated sense organs such as eyes and ears. But they are still deadly predators. Their method of attack, and defence, is the tiny stinging cells contained in their tentacles. Inside each cell is a capsule called a nematocyst, which contains a long, coiled thread. In some species these are barbed, in others they contain venom. Stimulated by touch or by certain chemicals, the threads flick out and then either the barbs hold on to the prey, or venom is injected into it. The animal then drags its victim into the digestive cavity, or stomach, within the body, to feast on its flesh. Some jellyfish have exceedingly powerful venom that can cause great pain if bathers brush against them. Nematocysts remain active for a time even after the animal is washed up and dies on the shore.

KRAKEN AHOY
The Kraken, a sea monster of Norse legend, made short work of ships and their crews. As is often the case, the fable has some basis in fact. The Kraken bears more than a passing resemblance to the squid, a member of the mollusc group. Atlantic giant squid have been recorded at 15 m (50 ft) long, including tentacles. However, unlike jellyfish tentacles, those of the squid do not possess stings. The squid hunts by grasping and grabbing its prey.

Common prawn

INSIDE AN ANEMONE
Anemones, and their cnidarian relatives, are simply constructed creatures. A ring of tentacles surrounds the mouth which leads to a digestive cavity inside the body. Prey is pushed into the cavity, digested and absorbed, and any remains excreted through the mouth.

Tentacles *Mouth*

Body cavity

Digestive cavity, or stomach

Foot

THE STINGING THREAD
Under the microscope it is possible to see tiny sting-containing cells on the tentacles of cnidarian animals. When the cell is triggered by touch or certain chemicals, its internal fluid pressure quickly increases. This forces the thread-like filament to shoot out. Some filaments are barbed; some contain the stinging venom; some are both barbed and venomous.

Coiled filament

Trigger hair

Discharged filament

Cell body

Cell nucleus

Undischarged nematocyst

Discharged nematocyst

PRAWN SNACK
This snakelocks anemone is in the process of capturing a common prawn and pulling it towards its mouth. The barbed stinging cells in the tentacles help to subdue the prey and paralyze it. When the prawn is drawn into the anemone's stomach, more stings will finish it off.

MICROSCOPIC STINGERS
Hydroids such as these *Obelia* are also cnidarians. These small anemone-like creatures grow in colonies. They form a furry coating on submerged seaweeds, rocks, and wood. Each individual has a stalk about as thick as cotton thread. Its stinging tentacles catch microscopic plants and animals.

Green
snakelocks
anemone

Anemone ejects
strings (acontia) of
stinging cells from its
mouth to defend itself

A feeding machine

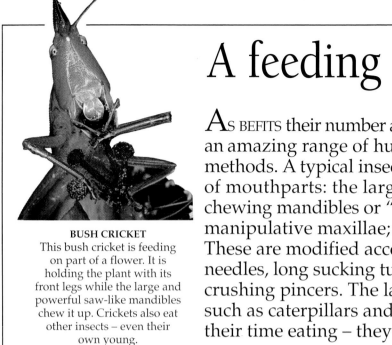

BUSH CRICKET
This bush cricket is feeding on part of a flower. It is holding the plant with its front legs while the large and powerful saw-like mandibles chew it up. Crickets also eat other insects – even their own young.

As BEFITS their number and variety, insects have an amazing range of hunting and feeding methods. A typical insect has three sets of mouthparts: the large biting and chewing mandibles or "jaws"; the smaller, manipulative maxillae; and the lip-like labia. These are modified according to diet into piercing needles, long sucking tubes, absorbent sponges, and crushing pincers. The larval stages of many insects, such as caterpillars and grubs, spend virtually all their time eating – they are living "eating machines".

FLEA BITES
This old engraving is not accurate, but it shows that fleas have a strong sucking tube surrounded by two pairs of palps, or sensory organs.

1 THE MEAL BEGINS
Large caterpillars, like this common mormon, always chew the edges of leaves. They grasp the leaf between their legs, stretch out their head in front, and then chew down towards the body with their mandibles. This action often produces a neat semicircular cut at the leaf edge.

Anal clasper

Starting out

Head

Shiny, green citrus leaf

2 STEADY PROGRESS
In addition to the three pairs of legs which all insects have on the thorax, caterpillars have four pairs of prolegs on the abdomen and a pair of anal claspers. Despite the long soft body, which is supported by these extra legs, a caterpillar has an external skeleton like other insects. When it is too big for its skin, it moults.

Head

True legs

After two hours

Anal clasper

Prolegs

INDIAN MOON MOTH LARVA
While chewing away the edges of leaves, Indian moon moth caterpillars are very exposed to predators. When touched, a caterpillar is liable to wriggle vigorously, and the pairs of spiny tubercles on its back will deter some birds from eating it.

Spiny, black and yellow tubercles deter predators

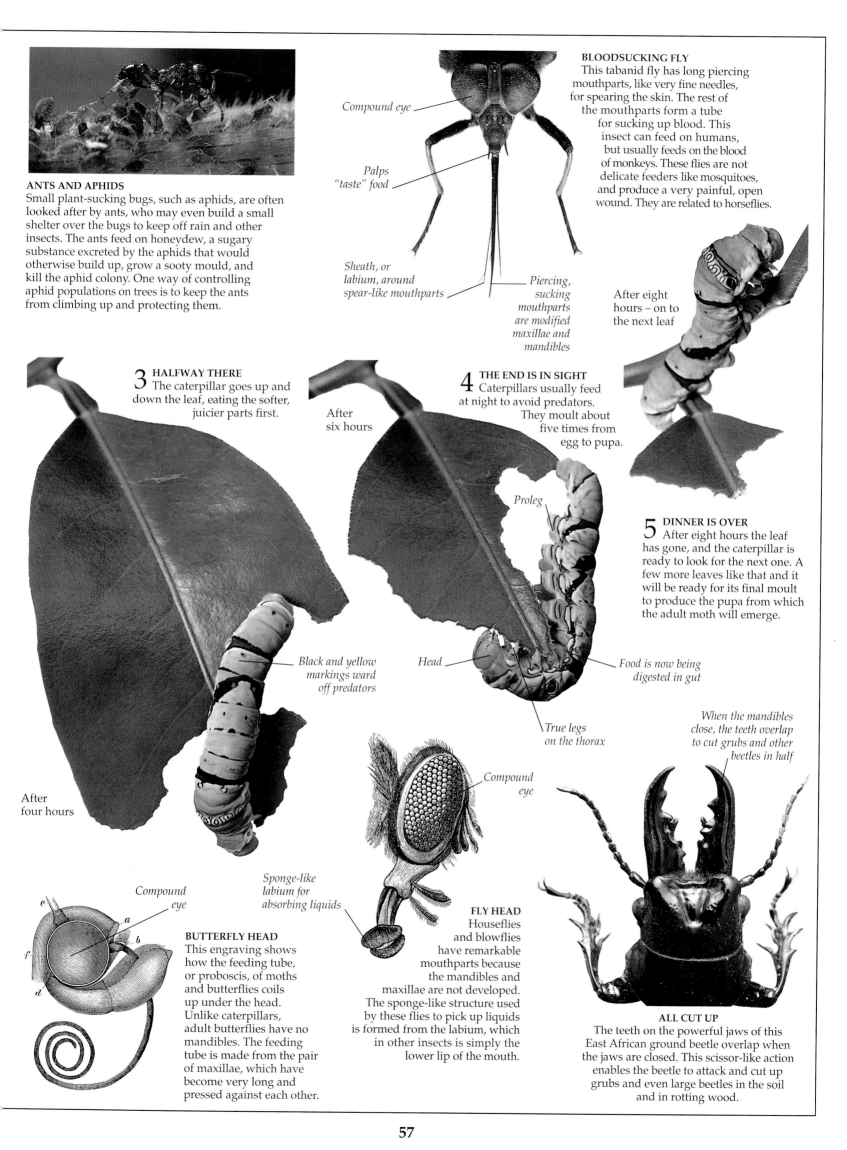

ANTS AND APHIDS
Small plant-sucking bugs, such as aphids, are often looked after by ants, who may even build a small shelter over the bugs to keep off rain and other insects. The ants feed on honeydew, a sugary substance excreted by the aphids that would otherwise build up, grow a sooty mould, and kill the aphid colony. One way of controlling aphid populations on trees is to keep the ants from climbing up and protecting them.

Compound eye

Palps "taste" food

Sheath, or labium, around spear-like mouthparts

Piercing, sucking mouthparts are modified maxillae and mandibles

BLOODSUCKING FLY
This tabanid fly has long piercing mouthparts, like very fine needles, for spearing the skin. The rest of the mouthparts form a tube for sucking up blood. This insect can feed on humans, but usually feeds on the blood of monkeys. These flies are not delicate feeders like mosquitoes, and produce a very painful, open wound. They are related to horseflies.

After eight hours – on to the next leaf

3 HALFWAY THERE
The caterpillar goes up and down the leaf, eating the softer, juicier parts first.

After six hours

4 THE END IS IN SIGHT
Caterpillars usually feed at night to avoid predators. They moult about five times from egg to pupa.

Proleg

5 DINNER IS OVER
After eight hours the leaf has gone, and the caterpillar is ready to look for the next one. A few more leaves like that and it will be ready for its final moult to produce the pupa from which the adult moth will emerge.

Black and yellow markings ward off predators

Head

Food is now being digested in gut

After four hours

True legs on the thorax

When the mandibles close, the teeth overlap to cut grubs and other beetles in half

Compound eye

Sponge-like labium for absorbing liquids

Compound eye

BUTTERFLY HEAD
This engraving shows how the feeding tube, or proboscis, of moths and butterflies coils up under the head. Unlike caterpillars, adult butterflies have no mandibles. The feeding tube is made from the pair of maxillae, which have become very long and pressed against each other.

FLY HEAD
Houseflies and blowflies have remarkable mouthparts because the mandibles and maxillae are not developed. The sponge-like structure used by these flies to pick up liquids is formed from the labium, which in other insects is simply the lower lip of the mouth.

ALL CUT UP
The teeth on the powerful jaws of this East African ground beetle overlap when the jaws are closed. This scissor-like action enables the beetle to attack and cut up grubs and even large beetles in the soil and in rotting wood.

Fishy food

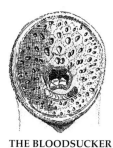

THE BLOODSUCKER
The jawless lamprey feeds by attaching itself to its prey with a sucker, then rasping away at the flesh with its teeth, and sucking the blood.

Almost 500 million years ago, fish were the first animals with a backbone. The earliest fish were jawless, with sucking mouthparts. About 440 million years ago, the group evolved the first true jaws. Invertebrates such as insects have jaw-like mouthparts (mandibles), but these usually work in a side-to-side fashion. True jaws are hinged and move up and down, worked by powerful muscles on the side of the head. Today, fish have adapted to an incredible array of foods and feeding methods. Large, crushing teeth indicate meals of shellfish, corals, or tough plant matter; sharp, pointed teeth indicate a hunting lifestyle; while a wide, gaping mouth shows a gulping method of feeding.

SKEWERED FISH
The popular notion of a swordfish with an unfortunate victim impaled on its sword is shown in this fanciful engraving. In reality, the sword may be used to jab or swipe sideways at prey.

Elephant-snout fish skull

Tiny jaws at end of "nose"

POKING ITS NOSE IN
The elephant-snout fish from Africa has a long, curved "nose" with tiny jaws at the end. It pokes these between stones, into cracks, and down into the mud, to find its food of small water creatures.

Pouting mouth for sucking in food

European bream skull

SURPRISING JAWS
Deep-bodied but extremely thin, the European John Dory creeps up on smaller fish and prawns. Its great jaws suddenly lever forwards and engulf the prey.

John Dory skull

CHEWING THROAT
The common or European bream, a silvery-olive freshwater fish, has a "pouting" mouth which it uses to sift and churn through the mud, sucking up small bottom-dwelling worms, shellfish, and insect larvae. These are then ground up by pharyngeal, or throat, teeth.

Pharyngeal teeth of bream

Lever mechanism thrusts jaws forwards

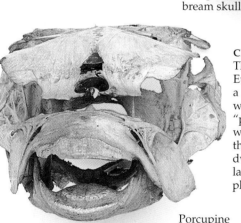

Porcupine fish skull

PRICKLES NO PROBLEM
The porcupine fish is well known for the ability to puff itself up and erect its spines when threatened. Lesser known is its diet, which consists of hard-shelled mussels and other shellfish, corals lurking in their stony homes, and even sea urchins hiding beneath their own spines. In each jaw, the teeth are fused to form a hard-edged biting ridge at the front, with a flat crushing plate behind.

The porcupine fish can crack hard-shelled mussels in its jaws

Strong, crushing teeth

Brazil nuts

FRUIT AND NUT CASE
The pacu, from the Amazon of Brazil, eats fruits and nuts that fall into the river. Its strong, crushing teeth are at the front of its mouth.

Prawn

Trumpetfish skull

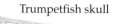

Seed of the piranha tree

TRUMPETFISH TWEEZERS
A long, rigid "beak" extends between the trumpetfish's small mouth and its eyes. The snout and the tiny teeth at the end are used like tweezers, to pick small aquatic animals out of their holes.

BEWARE THE BARRACUDA

Barracudas are fearsome predators of warmer oceans. They seize, maim, and tear up other fish with their formidable array of spear-like teeth. The larger barracudas, which grow to nearly 3 m (10ft) long, have been known to attack humans. However, many divers say the barracudas do not deserve their bad reputation. Although they may trail humans for some time, and they certainly look frightening enough, they rarely strike unless provoked.

Sharp triangular teeth lock together for a clean bite

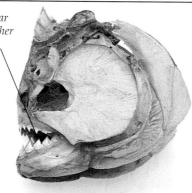

MOUTHFUL OF FANGS

The South American piranha, or piraya, has a mouthful of triangular, blade-like teeth. This river fish eats fruit and seeds as well as other fish. A group can soon devour larger prey by neatly chopping small pieces off it.

Sharp, dagger-like teeth at front tear prey's flesh

STONY FACED

When the stonefish lies on the sea bed it is camouflaged by its remarkably rock-like appearance. It then gulps in unwary prey with its wide upward-facing mouth.

Wide mouth on top of head

Stonefish skull

SHARP NOSE

Not a medieval sword, but the nose of the spectacular swordfish. The entire fish may be more than 4 m (13 ft) long; youngsters have a relatively short bill (snout) which lengthens into the flattened sword as they mature. No-one is sure exactly what the sword is used for. It may simply be a result of extreme stream-lining, the sword making the fish's progress faster.

CORAL CRUSHERS COMBINED

Coral reefs harbour an amazing variety of fish, which have a similarly amazing variety of feeding methods. The powerful, horny "beak" of the parrotfish is made of fused teeth. It uses this to scrape the thin layer of algae (seaweeds) and corals from rocks. This is then ground to a powder by strong pharyngeal plates. The drawn-out snout of the forceps fish is ideal for inserting into crannies and nooks for small bits of food. Both the triggerfish and the leather jacket's chisel-like teeth can bore holes in shells.

Horny beak

Coral

Leather jacket skull

Parrotfish skull

Triggerfish skull

Swordfish nose or "sword"

SURFACE SKIMMER

Called the halfbeak because the lower jaw is usually longer than the upper, this fish skims the undersurface of the water, swallowing plankton and larval fishes.

Forceps fish skull

CHAINSAW MASSACRE

This partly cutaway sawfish snout shows the "blades" of teeth in cartilage sockets. In fact this is a cartilaginous fish, a close relative of the sharks. Razor-sharp teeth on the saw can kill fish. It is also used for probing into the sea bed to dislodge food such as molluscs and crustaceans. The biggest sawfish are over 7 m (24 ft) long.

Sawfish snout

Sharp saw teeth in cartilage sockets

Jaws of death

LIKE BONY FISH, the cartilaginous fish, such as sharks, continually lose their old teeth and grow new ones. In bony fish, new teeth develop in the gum or jaw, below the old ones. But in sharks, when the front teeth wear out they are replaced by new ones growing in another row behind them. An individual shark can get through thousands of teeth in a lifetime. As the shark grows, its new teeth are larger than the ones they replace. Sharks' teeth come in many shapes according to what kind of food they eat. Teeth shaped like small spikes are used for gripping small prey. Serrated teeth are used for cutting. Long, curved teeth get hold of slippery fish. Blunt teeth crunch up shellfish. A few species of shark, such as basking and whale sharks, have tiny teeth compared to their great size. They do not use their teeth to feed, but instead filter food out of the water.

Tiny teeth of basking shark

Gill rakers

MOUTH WIDE OPEN
Basking sharks swim along with their mouths open to catch shrimps and other small creatures, called plankton, that drift in the sea. The food is trapped on rows of bristles called gill rakers as the water flows through the mouth and out through the gill slits. The gill rakers are shed each year during the winter months when there is little food about. A new set of rakers grows in the spring and then the basking sharks can start to feed again.

EPAULETTE EATING
Epaulette sharks live on coral reefs in the southwest Pacific Ocean around Australia and Papua New Guinea. They grow to about 1 m (3.3 ft) long and can crawl along the bottom using their pectoral fins. These sharks search among the shallows and rockpools for small fish, crabs, shrimps, and other small creatures to eat.

Epaulette eating

SMILE PLEASE
Swell sharks (top right) from the eastern Pacific Ocean have big mouths for their 1 m (3.3 ft) length. Armed with rows of tiny teeth, these sharks eat bony fish which they ambush at night while the fish rest on the sea bed. Only the rows of small front teeth of the Port Jackson (bottom right) are visible when its mouth is open. At the back of its jaws are strong, flat teeth for crushing shelled prey.

Mouth of a swell shark

CRUNCHY DIET
Port Jackson sharks have small, pointed front teeth to grasp their prey. The strong, flat back teeth can crunch through hard-shelled crabs, mussels (right), and sea urchins (below right).

Section through a Port Jackson's jaws

Mouth of a Port Jackson

TIGER MOUTH

Tiger sharks cruise the warm waters of the world around islands and coasts of continents, and often move in-shore at night to feed.

ALL THE BETTER TO EAT WITH

A tiger shark's strong teeth can crunch through a turtle's bones and shell. If a tooth breaks, it is replaced by one growing forwards from the row behind. As in all sharks, the teeth are larger, stronger versions of the tiny pointed placoid scales on the shark's skin.

DAILY MENU

Tiger sharks eat all kinds of food from squishy jellyfish to tough shelled turtles. They are not put off by the jellyfish's stings or even venom from sea snakes which they also eat. Sea birds are not safe as tiger sharks will grab them from the surface of the sea. Carcasses of land animals such as chickens, dogs, horses, and cows which have washed into the sea, are also eaten. Even tin cans, coal, and plastic bags have been found in their stomachs.

Sea turtle

Jellyfish

JAWS

The jaws of a tiger shark are only loosely connected by ligaments and muscles to the rest of its skull, so it can push its jaws out to take a big bite. When it feeds on large prey, it shakes its head back and forth to tear off chunks.

DISH OF THE DAY

Sand tigers eat a variety of bony fish (left), as well as lobsters, small sharks, and rays.

Goatfish

Lobster

RAGGED TOOTH SHARK

Sand tigers, called ragged tooth sharks in South Africa and grey nurse sharks in Australia, reach 3 m (10 ft) in length. Their long, curved teeth get progressively smaller from the middle to the sides of the jaw and are ideal for snaring fish or squid. The sharks look fierce, but will attack only if provoked.

Cunning carnivores

SNAKE SNACK
Many amphibians are the favourite food of birds, mammals, fish, insects, spiders, and even other amphibians! This French earthenware plate, c. 1560, shows a frog about to be eaten by one of its main enemies – a grass snake.

THE VAST MAJORITY of amphibians are carnivores. They capture their prey by a variety of cunning hunting methods, and eat almost any live food that they can manage to swallow or gulp down. Insects, spiders, snails, slugs, and earthworms form the main part of the diet for most adult amphibians. Larger species, like the ornate horned toad, will take larger prey, maybe even a rat, while some species are cannibals – a case of frog eat frog. There are also specialist feeders – some smaller frogs and toads eat only ants or termites, and one species of Brazilian treefrog eats only berries. All amphibians will gorge themselves if food is plentiful, to enable them to survive times when food is scarce.

Frog launching itself towards prey

1 LEAP AND SNAP FEEDING
Frogs are more active feeders than toads and will not often sit and wait for their prey – "see it and seize it" is their strategy. Launching itself towards a woodlouse, this frog has to judge the distance it needs to jump, and when to open its mouth, with split-second accuracy.

Woodlouse

2 READY FOR PREY
As the frog leaps, it opens its mouth, ready to catch the woodlouse with its long, sticky tongue. Frogs usually snap up fast-moving insects, like flies, crickets, and grasshoppers. The frog gets only one chance – if it misses it will have wasted its energy. The slow-moving woodlouse might fall or get knocked off its leaf and escape, if the frog mistimes its jump.

European common frog going after prey

Legs and body at full stretch

Eyes open

A BIG MOUTHFUL . . .
The ornate horned toad's huge mouth, sit-and-wait feeding method, and camouflaged body markings help it take large, passing insects, mice, and other amphibians by surprise. When a horned toad opens its mouth, the whole of the front end of its body seems to open up!

SLOW, SLOW, QUICK . . .

Newts, salamanders, and caecilians tend to eat slow-moving, soft-bodied animals, like this earthworm. They approach their prey slowly, then make a quick, last-minute grab, often turning their head on one side. They grip the food using teeth in their upper and lower jaws.

Eyelid starting to close

Woodlouse

Mandarin salamander eating an earthworm

Tongue flips out from front of mouth

Sticky tip of tongue

3 SUCCESSFUL STRIKE
With the precision of a guided missile homing in on its target, the frog's tongue flips out of the open mouth and strikes the woodlouse.

Making a meal of a mealworm

Watching its prey

TONGUE FLIPS

The boy's party whistle flips open and forwards because air is blown into it. The tongue of a frog or toad flips out and over, because muscles in the floor of the mouth push the tongue forwards.

SEE IT, WATCH IT, EAT IT

Toads are careful, deliberate feeders. This common toad's attention has been attracted by a wriggling mealworm. It turns its head towards its prey, watching it intently. Some toads may even stalk their prey using creeping, cat-like movements. Suddenly, leaning over the mealworm, the toad gives a rapid tongue-flick, and the mealworm disappears.

Ready for action

Tongue flicks out

Eyes firmly shut as ornate horned toad swallows its prey

. . . TAKES SOME SWALLOWING

The blinking of the eye pushes the eyeball down, increases the pressure in the mouth, and helps the toad swallow its meal.

. . . and mealworm disappears

All but the tail has disappeared

Toad swallows, blinking its eyes

Reptilian repast

SLOW BUT SURE
Very few tortoises or turtles have the speed or agility to catch fast-moving prey. As a result, most feed on vegetation, or on slow-moving animals, such as molluscs, worms, and insect larvae. They all make the most of food that is nearby and then move to the next feeding area. As well as fleshy plants, the spur-thighed tortoise also enjoys the occasional morsel of any dead animal it finds.

MOST REPTILES ARE MEAT EATERS. Crocodiles and snakes are all carnivores, and have perfected methods of eating their food, but some snakes have specialized diets, including birds' eggs and fish eggs (eaten by some sea snakes). Many of the lizards are also predators, feeding on insects, mammals, birds, and other reptiles. The Komodo dragon has serrated teeth rather like a shark's, which it uses to cut flesh from prey as big as water buffalos. Among the lizards, large iguanas and some of the bigger skinks are mostly vegetarian. Tortoises eat a variety of plants, but even they occasionally eat meat. Freshwater turtles often eat worms, snails, fish, and other small animals. Sea turtles generally feed on jellyfish, crabs, molluscs, and fish, but they also eat plants.

HOOK MEETS HIS END
In J.M. Barrie's *Peter Pan*, Hook is haunted by the crocodile who has already eaten his hand – and is looking for more! Helped for a time by a clock that ticks in the creature's stomach, Hook is finally tricked and eaten.

CROCODILE LARDER
Nile crocodiles occasionally share the carcass of a large animal such as a wildebeest or a buffalo. Crocodile stomachs are only the size of a basketball, so crocodiles cannot eat a big animal all at once. Prey is often, therefore, hidden wedged under an old log or boulder to be finished off later. This has led to the mistaken belief that crocodiles like to eat meat that is "high". In fact, they prefer fresh meat.

Armlets

Pieces of turtle shell

Stones

Bangles

Porcupine quills

STOMACH STORE
Crocodiles often devour hard, heavy objects, such as stones and pieces of metal. One can only hope that no-one was wearing the bangle when it was swallowed! The objects may be eaten to weigh down the crocodile, so it floats low in the water, or perhaps to help the crocodile digest its food.

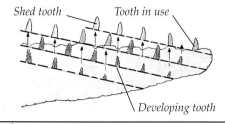

Shed tooth   Tooth in use

Developing tooth

DEVELOPING TEETH
Crocodiles and other reptiles shed their teeth throughout their lives, with new ones constantly replacing the old ones. The developing teeth grow up through the holes of those already in use.

Eyed lizards are mainly ground-dwellers, but are also excellent climbers. Crickets and grasshoppers are their favourite food

CRISPY CRICKET

After a rapid chase, the eyed lizard grabs a cricket with its jaws, and shakes its victim violently to stun it. It passes the cricket to the back of its mouth, its jaws moving over the prey in a succession of snapping movements. The lizard's teeth grip and release the cricket as the jaws are raised and lowered. It is important that the lizard moves fast – the cricket may not yet be totally stunned and will not waste an opportunity to try to escape. The majority of lizards are insect eaters and in some areas are important in keeping insect populations down.

SHARPSHOOTERS

With a tongue as long as their body and tail, chameleons have been described as the sharp-shooters of the lizards. The tongue is hollow and unforked with a large, sticky tip, and can be shot from the mouth by a contracting muscle at lightning speed and with tremendous accuracy. A second set of muscles is used to draw the tongue back into the mouth, where it is kept bunched up until it is needed again.

A specialist snake

MOST GROUPS of animals have their specialist feeders, adapted to a very limited type of food. Among the reptiles, perhaps the most extraordinary is the African egg-eating snake. Many snakes eat eggs as part of a varied diet, but the egg-eater eats exclusively eggs. Small eggs, especially the soft-shelled ones laid by lizards and some other snakes, are easy to eat, as they can be quickly slit open by the snake's teeth. Larger, hard-shelled eggs, such as those laid by birds, need special treatment. True egg-eating snakes eat only birds' eggs, which they swallow whole as they have few teeth. They have tooth-like spines that stick down from the backbone and crack open the egg as it passes down to the snake's throat.

Diet of eggs

One problem with an egg diet is that food is not always available. In some parts of the world, birds lay their eggs only at certain times of the year, and so an egg-eating snake may have to go for a long time without food. Fortunately, egg-eating snakes can bring up, or regurgitate, egg shell. This means that no space is wasted in the snake's stomach, and it can eat as many eggs as it finds. Nor does the snake waste vital energy in passing the shell through its digestive system.

2 SWALLOW HARD
The jaws "unhinge" so the egg can pass between them and down into the snake's throat. The skin on the side of the neck is very elastic, and at this stage the egg is still unbroken.

Head arched down, pushing egg against bony inner spines to puncture shell

Finely interlinked scales, which separate as skin stretches

3 SPINY BONES
The passage of the egg has now been stopped by the tooth-like spines on the underside of the neck bones. These protrude into the oesophagus (gullet) and crack or slice open the egg shell.

A valve at the entrance to the stomach accepts yolks and liquids, but rejects pieces of shell

The "bulge" is noticeably smaller

4 GOING DOWN....
Once the egg is punctured, the muscles of the snake's body work in waves to squeeze out the contents, which then continue on to the stomach. The snake now bends its body into S-shaped curves, forcing the collapsed shell back towards the mouth.

5 AND UP IT COMES.........
It may take from five minutes to an hour, depending on the size of the egg, for it to be completely swallowed. Finally, the snake gapes widely and the compacted cigar-shaped shell is brought up. The fragments of shell are still held together by the sticky egg membranes.

The jagged edges of the shell pieces are stuck together. All the goodness in the egg has been drained and swallowed

Regurgitated shell

1 TOO GREEDY?

An African egg-eater is about to swallow an egg. It looks impossible – the egg is twice the width of the snake's body. The snake has a lightly-built skull and the mouth is lined with sticky ridges.

Mouth ridges grip the egg as it passes towards the snake's throat

Because of its shape, an egg is remarkably resistant to crushing before it is pierced by the snake's bony spines

STOP! THIEF!

The monitor lizards, which include some of the giants of the reptilian world, are well known for their greed. Many live on the carcasses of dead animals and on live animals – but even a nest of eggs is not safe with them around.

Bird beaks, big and small

MILLIONS OF YEARS AGO, birds lost their teeth. They were too heavy for their low-weight airborne lifestyle. The teeth have been replaced by the beak, or bill, made of the lightweight substance keratin, like your fingernails. The beak covers the jaw bones inside it. Bird beaks have evolved an endless variety of shapes and sizes, adapted mainly to various food items, but also to other aspects of the bird's life, such as preening its feathers, defending itself against enemies, and displaying to mates at breeding time.

Thrush

Eating plants and seeds

Birds that eat plants and seeds have to crush their food before they can digest it. As they have no teeth, they do this with powerful beaks and also with the gizzard – a muscular "grinding chamber" in the stomach.

Finch skull

Hard-cased seeds

Goose skull

SPECIALIST SEED-EATERS
Finches, which number more than 150 species, have short, sharp bills for breaking open seeds and nuts. Amazingly, some finches have bills which can exert more crushing force than a human hand.

Leaf crops

Cultivated grain

Pigeon skull

FEEDING ON CROPS
Pigeons and doves originally ate the leaves and seeds of wild plants. Now they often feed on cultivated ones as well. They can also use their pointed bills like a straw when drinking – a unique ability among birds.

LIVING ON GRASS
Geese are among the few kinds of bird that can live on a diet of grass. But geese digest grass poorly, and it passes through their body in just two hours. Because they get so little out of their food, they must eat a lot of it, and so feed almost constantly.

Capercaillie skull

Powerful hooked beak for grasping leaves from trees and crushing seeds

Broad bill for tearing grass

ALL-ROUND PLANT-EATERS
Game birds – species such as pheasants, grouse, and this capercaillie from northern Europe – eat whatever plant food is available, although their preference is for seeds. In winter, the capercaillie lives on the leaves of coniferous trees, a source of food which few other animals can utilize. It pulls the leaves from branches with its powerful hooked beak.

Seeds

Needle-shaped leaves of conifer trees

The grass and waterplants on which geese feed

Invertebrate eaters

Every spring, the number of insects and other invertebrates (animals without backbones) increases dramatically. These animals form the food for many species of migratory birds. In winter, the supply is much smaller and food is harder to find, consisting mainly of worms and insect larvae (grubs) in woods or in the soil. These are sought out by specialist insect-eating birds.

Blackcap skull

Aphids

Caterpillar

THE SNAIL-SMASHER
Thrushes eat a wide range of food – both plant and animal. Some feed on snails, which they smash open on stone "anvils".

Thrush skull

PROBING WARBLERS
These small songsters use their probing beaks to pick insects from leaves and bark. When the supply dries up in early autumn, they migrate southwards.

Centipedes

Snail shells broken open by thrush

Woodpecker skull

LARGE INSECT EATERS
Birds like woodpeckers and the mainly ground-feeding hoopoe use their beak to pick large insects out of crevices in trees. Woodpeckers also chisel into the wood to find concealed grubs. Their extremely long tongues have spear-like tips which are used for impaling their prey.

Beetle larvae

Adult beetle

A DIET OF WORMS
Earthworms are eaten not only by garden birds, but also by some owls and other birds of prey.

Pecked apple

Hoopoe skull

Ribbonworm, or ragworm

Silt-burrowing lugworm

Avocet feeding

Feeding on the shore

Although there are very few saltwater insects, the seashore contains a year-round supply of other invertebrates for birds to eat, from crabs and shellfish to burrowing worms.

Avocet skull

THE SWEEP-NET BEAK
The avocet catches worms and other prey by striding forwards and sweeping its beak from side to side in the water on the surface of the sand or mud. It is one of the very few birds with an upturned beak.

Marine worms

Crab broken open and eaten; the hard skeleton is usually discarded

Cockle

Oystercatcher skull

A BUILT-IN HAMMER
The oystercatcher feeds on seashore animals with hard shells. It has a long beak like the avocet but, instead of ending in a fine point, its tip is blunt. This "built-in hammer" enables the oystercatcher to smash through the shells of its prey. This kind of feeding needs considerable skill, and some oystercatchers prize shells open instead. An experienced bird will know precisely where the weak points are on a mussel or cockle shell and, if it is lying on sand, the bird will carry the shell to a rock to break it open.

Tellins

Mussel

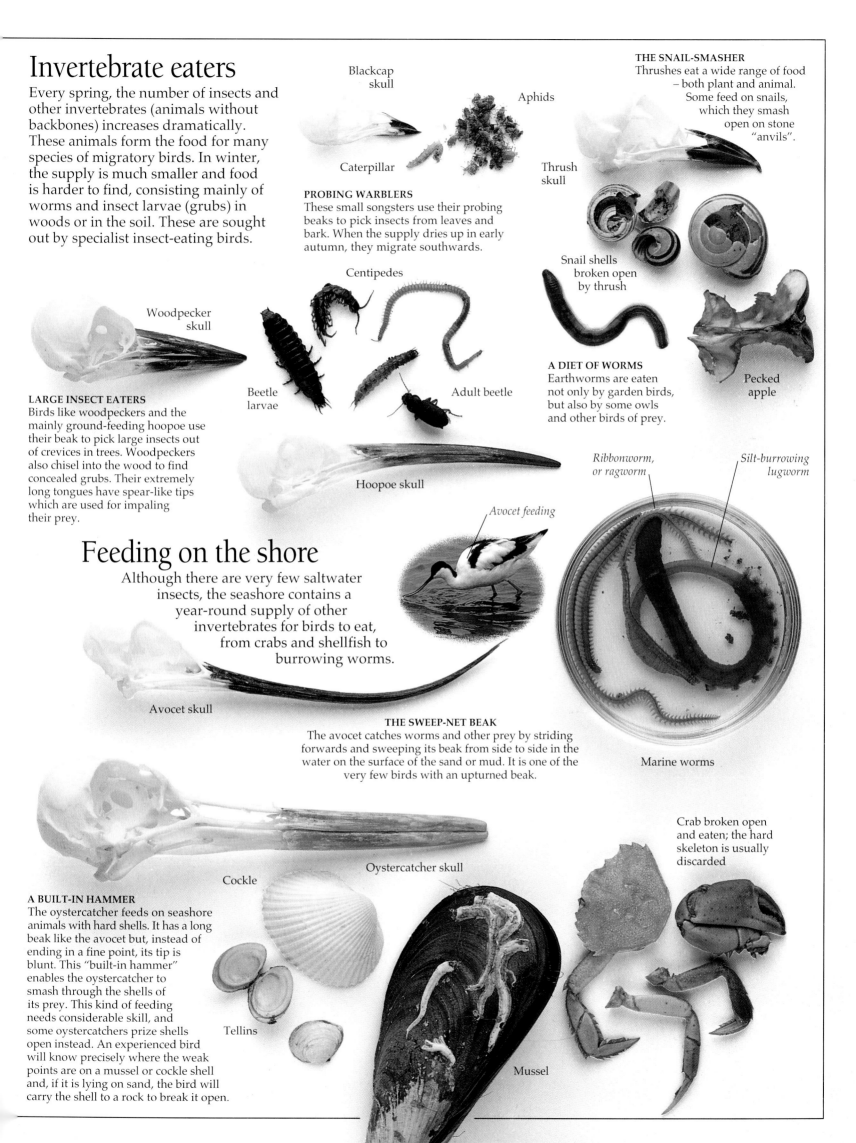

Beaks of hunting birds

FLIGHT ENABLES birds to cover long distances in search of food. This gives them a great advantage as predators, because few animals – on land or far out at sea – are beyond their reach. Flight also makes birds very effective all-round feeders. A dead animal, an unprotected nest, or a field of ripening crops is quickly spotted by passing birds and turned into a satisfying meal.

Kingfishers

Meat and fish eaters

Birds that feed on larger animals and fish catch their prey in two different ways. Most fish eaters use their beak to catch their quarry while, on land, birds of prey use their talons for catching and their beak for tearing.

Strips of meat torn from prey with powerful, hooked beak

Tawny owl skull

Fur is swallowed and later regurgitated as pellets

NIGHT AND DAY HUNTERS
Most owls hunt by night, using their huge eyes and astonishingly sensitive ears to locate prey such as mice, voles, and insects. As dawn breaks, the owls retire to rest, and birds of prey such as hawks and buzzards take over the hunting roles.

Buzzard skull

Large forward-pointing eyes enable the gannet to pinpoint fish below

Halves of the beak meet at a long straight line for holding fish before they are swallowed

Streamlined point for diving

ABOVE AND BELOW WATER
Gannets dive-bomb shoals of fish such as mackerel by plunging, with their wings folded, from heights of up to 30 m (100 ft). They stay below the surface for only a few seconds. Cormorants pursue fish under water. Their feathers do not trap air like those of other waterbirds, and this enables them to dive swiftly and overtake their prey.

Gannet skull

PATIENCE REWARDED
The heron fishes by stealth, staying motionless until its prey swims within reach of its long stabbing beak.

Hooked beak for grasping fish

Cormorant skull

Mackerel

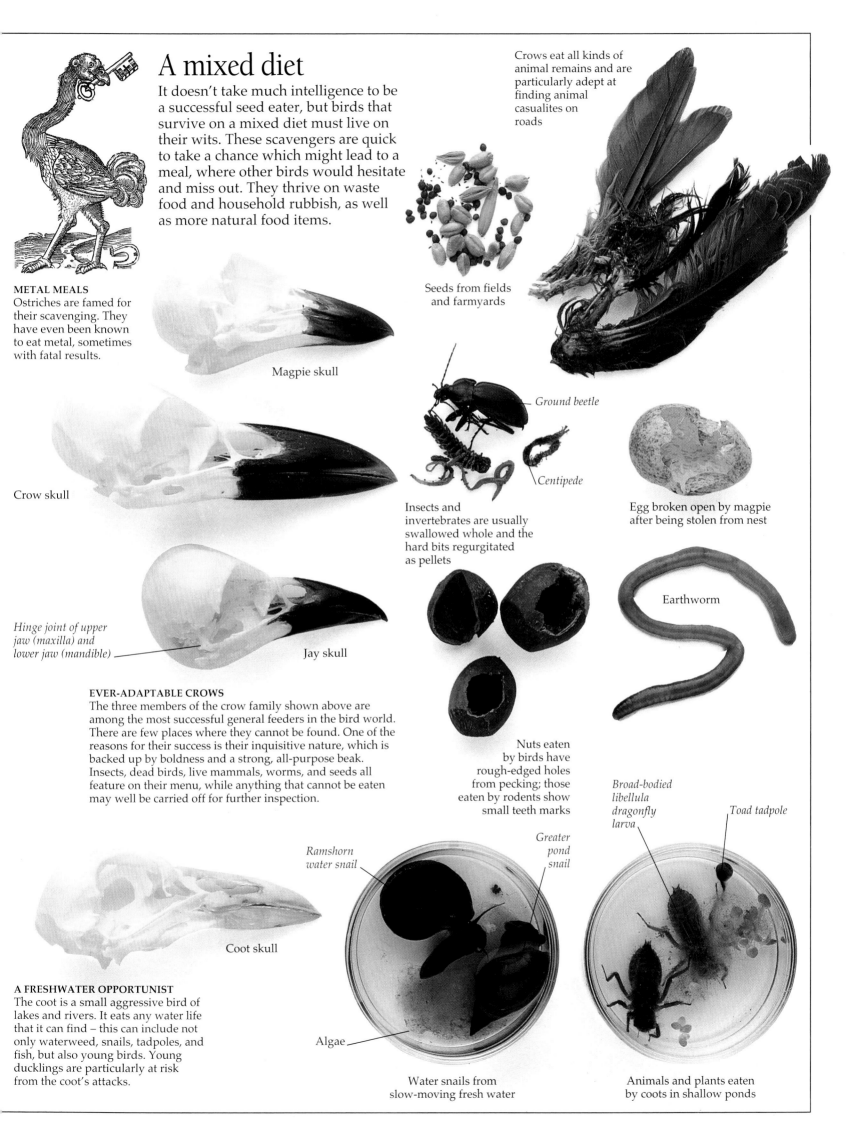

A mixed diet

It doesn't take much intelligence to be a successful seed eater, but birds that survive on a mixed diet must live on their wits. These scavengers are quick to take a chance which might lead to a meal, where other birds would hesitate and miss out. They thrive on waste food and household rubbish, as well as more natural food items.

Crows eat all kinds of animal remains and are particularly adept at finding animal casualites on roads

Seeds from fields and farmyards

METAL MEALS
Ostriches are famed for their scavenging. They have even been known to eat metal, sometimes with fatal results.

Magpie skull

Ground beetle

Centipede

Insects and invertebrates are usually swallowed whole and the hard bits regurgitated as pellets

Egg broken open by magpie after being stolen from nest

Crow skull

Hinge joint of upper jaw (maxilla) and lower jaw (mandible)

Jay skull

Earthworm

EVER-ADAPTABLE CROWS
The three members of the crow family shown above are among the most successful general feeders in the bird world. There are few places where they cannot be found. One of the reasons for their success is their inquisitive nature, which is backed up by boldness and a strong, all-purpose beak. Insects, dead birds, live mammals, worms, and seeds all feature on their menu, while anything that cannot be eaten may well be carried off for further inspection.

Nuts eaten by birds have rough-edged holes from pecking; those eaten by rodents show small teeth marks

Broad-bodied libellula dragonfly larva

Toad tadpole

Greater pond snail

Ramshorn water snail

Coot skull

A FRESHWATER OPPORTUNIST
The coot is a small aggressive bird of lakes and rivers. It eats any water life that it can find – this can include not only waterweed, snails, tadpoles, and fish, but also young birds. Young ducklings are particularly at risk from the coot's attacks.

Algae

Water snails from slow-moving fresh water

Animals and plants eaten by coots in shallow ponds

Teeth for the job

ALL GROUPS OF ANIMALS have differently shaped teeth and jaws, adapted to various foods. These adaptations reach their greatest variety in mammals, who have teeth made of hard, tough enamel. Long, thin jaws, with small teeth toward the front are good at probing and nibbling small foods such as berries or insects. Short, broad jaws, with large premolar and molar teeth near the back, are useful for grinding tough plants or cracking bone and gristle. Long, spear-like canine teeth at the front sides of the mouth, for stabbing and tearing, are the hallmarks of a hunting mammal.

Coypu skull

Coypu

NON-STOP GNAWING
A rodent's front teeth never stop growing, but they are worn down continuously by use. The gap in the tooth row allows the lips to seal off the inside of the mouth when gnawing.

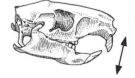

Lower jaw moves up and down

UNGULATES
The lower jawbone of ungulates (mammals with hooves) is generally deep at the back, giving a large area to anchor the strong chewing muscle. Special jaw joints allow sideways movement of the jaws as well as up-and-down chewing. All ungulates are herbivorous.

Goat skull

Position of horny pad

Deep lower jaw for muscle attachment

Molar and premolar grinders

Gap allows tongue to manipulate bulky food

Lower jaw moves from side to side and back and forth

PULLING OFF A MOUTHFUL
Some ungulates, like the goat, have no top front teeth. The goat pulls at food using its tough tongue and lips, its padded upper gums, and small lower incisors (missing from this specimen). Its jaws also slide front to back for even better grinding.

Position of lower incisors

Goat

72

OMNIVORES

Omnivorous mammals (those that eat anything) include primates – the monkeys and apes, and ourselves. The jaws and teeth have no extreme specializations. Incisors, canines, premolars, and molars are all much the same size.

Chimpanzee

Chimpanzee skull

← →

Limited sideways movement

Lower jaw moves up and down

Temporalis muscle attaches here

Deep flange for chewing muscle

Enlarged canines

OUR CLOSEST RELATIVE

The chimp's jaws and teeth are similar to a human's, but larger in proportion to its skull. They mainly slice and chew, since the hands gather the food. The chimp's jaw joint is more rigid than a human's, so the animal cannot chew with such a large side-to-side movement as we can. Because of this its teeth are worn into a pattern of high points and cusps, in contrast to the more rounded human teeth.

CARNIVORES

Lions, tigers and other cats, wolves, coyotes and other dogs, and mustelids such as weasels, stoats, and badgers all belong to the mammal group called the Carnivora. Their front incisor teeth are relatively small; their canine teeth are large, pointed fangs; and their premolar and molar teeth are carnassials, with sharp ridges for slicing gristle and sinew.

Lion skull

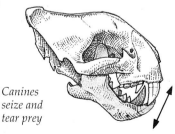

Canines seize and tear prey

Lower jaw moves up and down only

Lion

SKULL OF THE KING

The lion has a massive cheek ridge of bone. The huge masseter muscle runs from here to the lower jaw, for crushing power when the mouth is almost closed. The fearsome front canine teeth have deep roots for strength when holding on as the prey struggles.

Masseter muscle attaches here

Carnassial teeth shear past each other to cut up meat

Champion herbivore

A THORNY PROBLEM
The sharp, finger-length thorns of acacia trees are no defence against an elephant. Carefully avoiding the thorns with her trunk, this African elephant has torn off a branch and is crushing off the bark with her molars.

MOST MAMMALS, INCLUDING HUMANS, have two sets of teeth in their lifetime. By the time a human stops growing, at about 20 years of age, he or she will have a complete second set of teeth, although the last molars, or wisdom teeth, sometimes take longer. A 20-year-old elephant, on the other hand, will already be well into its fourth set of cheek teeth. There are six sets of four in total, but at any one time, only one set is functional. Each set consists of two cheek teeth in each jaw, one on each side. As the elephant grows, each new set of teeth moves into place, and is slightly bigger than the last set. The teeth do not erupt from above in the top jaw and from below in the bottom jaw, as in humans, but move along the jaw from the back towards the front. Each tooth gets more and more worn as it moves forwards, but by the time the last bits drop out, it has been completely replaced by the tooth behind it, rather as if the teeth were on a very slow conveyor belt. These successive sets of teeth are responsible for chewing and grinding more food than any other animal – an adult elephant consumes up to 200 kg (440 lb) of grasses, leaves, twigs, fruits, and other plant food each day.

JAWBONE
This left half of an African elephant's jawbone has had the bone chipped away to reveal the roots of the teeth. The big tooth is molar 5, but the last bit of molar 4 is still in use. The round lump in the angle of the jaw is the beginning of molar 6.

Molar 6

Molar 5 is good for about 20 years of chewing

Roots deep in jawbone

Human molar

African elephant molar has diamond-shaped ridges

Asian elephant molar has parallel ridges

TEETH RIDGES
An elephant molar is made up of several plates, or lamellae, stuck together. The enamel top of each molar wears down as it grinds on its opposite tooth, revealing a diamond shape in African elephants, and thin parallel ridges in Asian elephants.

Molar 6

The last molar is bigger than a brick and appears when the elephant is about 40 years old

SET OF TEETH
When an elephant dies, the size of its teeth, and the amount of wear on them, enable scientists to work out how long it lived. These six teeth come from five different African elephants, ranging from a tiny calf to an adult of more than 50 years.

Molar 5

Molar 4

Molar 3

Molar 2

Molar 1

Only the first five ridges of molar 5 have come into use

Molar 4 is almost worn out. It comes from the same elephant as molar 5

Molar 3 usually lasts from about three and a half to about nine years of age

Molar 2 usually erupts before the age of 18 months

Molar 1 is present in newborn baby elephants

Root of mammoth tooth

MAMMOTH TOOTH
Fossil mammoth teeth are sometimes dredged up from the bottom of the North Sea. The ridges on the grinding surface are more like those of an Asian elephant than an African.

The underside
of the trunk is
the elephant's
upper lip

OPEN WIDE
The upper right molar is visible in
this Asian elephant's mouth. The ridges
on the grinding surface run across the
tooth, and so the elephant chews with a
forwards and backwards circular motion
of the lower jaw. In most other animals,
ridges run along the length of the teeth –
which is why cattle move their jaws
from side to side. The elephant's tusks
are its upper incisors – its only front
teeth. They grow continuously and
do not normally wear out.

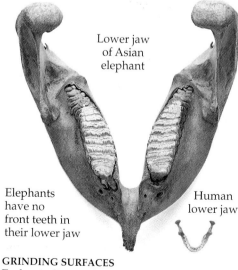

Lower jaw
of Asian
elephant

Elephants
have no
front teeth in
their lower jaw

Human
lower jaw

GRINDING SURFACES
Each grinding surface in an adult human jaw
contains five teeth, and so humans grind with
20 teeth. The elephant's grinding surface is
just one massive molar, except when parts of
two teeth are in use during a tooth change.
Therefore, adult elephants grind with from
four to eight teeth at any one time.

The bottom lip
is pointed, and
each side folds
inwards, partially
enclosing the fleshy
pink tongue

ELEPHANT LITTER
Elephants select the
best parts of each
food plant. These roots
have been sheared off by
an African elephant's molars,
and discarded as it walked
along munching grasses,
leaves, and stems.

Dealing with a meal

THE FOOD OF SOME MAMMALS comes in convenient ready-to-eat form, for immediate consumption. Grass, leaves, and insects are instant prepackaged snacks. But other sources of food are more difficult to gather, or more awkward to manipulate. The mammals that rely on them need the bodily equivalent of shopping bags, can-openers, crowbars, and knives and forks to deal with their meal. For example, acorns and nuts are bursting with nutrients, but they are packaged in a strong, hard case which is tough to crack. The long, ever-growing, chisel-sharp incisor teeth of rodents are especially suited to gnawing, chipping, and levering open nuts. It's a successful approach – rodents make up one-quarter of all mammal species.

GRASPING TONGUE
The giraffe is an ungulate, or hoofed mammal. It is the tallest land animal at more than 5 m (17 ft) tall, so it can reach high up in the trees for its food. It can reach 30 cm (1 ft) higher by sticking out its long black tongue, like a grabbing hand, to pull leaves into its mouth. Then the long canine teeth strip the leaves from the twigs.

CHISELLING TEETH
In autumn and winter, the brown squirrel feeds mainly on nuts such as oak acorns, beech mast, and hazel cobs. The squirrel rolls the nut in its forepaws until it is the right way up, then applies the tremendous levering force of its sharp front teeth to a certain weak spot. The nut case then splits open. Young squirrels are born with a certain amount of case-cracking knowledge, but they refine the technique with practice.

BULGING CHEEKS
The golden hamster is a well-known pet. Like the wild hamster and many other rodent relatives, it collects food when it is abundant and "caches" it – stores it in a hidden place. The hamster's cheek pouches work like shopping bags.

Cheek pouches are empty

*Heading off to
a secret store*

*Mouse is alert
to danger, even
when feeding*

NIBBLING TEETH
In the wild, most mice have
a varied diet – seeds and fruits,
leaves and shoots, insects and other small
creatures, and mushrooms and other fungi.
However, evolution equipped the mouse as a
gramnivore, or grain eater. The mouse nibbles at
seeds and nuts with its typical rodent's incisors,
holding small items in its front paws. House mice,
such as these shown here, are even more versatile
than their wild cousins. They gnaw paper, string, soap,
candle wax, and many other household substances.

*Mice sit on
their back legs
when holding
food in their
front paws*

HOLDING HANDS
The otter rarely eats its catch of fish
in the water. It comes to the river
bank and holds down the slippery
meal with its front feet while tearing
at the flesh with its sharp, spear-like
canine teeth. Otters also eat small
mammals, birds, and frogs.

HOOKING CLAWS
The Malayan sun bear is the
smallest of the seven species
of bear. Its long, curved claws
are multi-purpose tools. In
addition to providing the grip for
climbing, they can hook fruit from
branches, tear bark off trunks to get at
grubs, and rip open the nests of termites, ants,
and bees to eat the occupants or steal the honey.

MASSAGING PAWS
The hamster quickly crams as much
food as possible into its cheeks.
Then it heads back to its burrow to
unpack the pouches by massaging
the items out with its front paws.
This strategy reduces the time
that this small, fairly defenceless
animal would otherwise spend
out in the open, chewing and
swallowing the food. In the
wild, a single hamster has
been known to amass nuts
and other food weighing
more than an adult human.

*Pouches
beginning
to extend*

Full pouches

Supreme hunter

OF ALL THE MAMMALS, those which rely on fresh meat the most, and follow the hunting lifestyle most completely, are the felids – the 35 or so species in the cat family. They range from enormous tigers, weighing over 350 kg (660 lb), and with a body 3 m (10 ft) long, to the black-footed cat of southern Africa, smaller than most pet cats. All cats are solitary predators, except for the lion which hunts in a family group, or pride. Cats usually kill victims smaller than themselves. Motionless animals sometimes escape attack, but with practice, cats can recognize prey by sound and scent alone. They have an excellent memory for places and will return many times to a spot where they once had successful hunting. Most cats stalk their prey, sometimes for a long time, then with a sudden rush, leap on it and sink their sharp canine teeth into the neck. Small cats feed mostly on mice, birds, lizards, beetles, and any other small animals they can catch. Large cats, like the leopard, feed on bigger animals about the size of a goat, and often drag their prey up into trees to keep it away from other predators.

TOM AND JERRY
In the famous cartoon, quickwitted Jerry the mouse often gets the better of the swashbuckling but slightly stupid Tom – not often the case in real life.

A stalking cat holds its body close to the ground

The pads on a cat's paws help it to move silently

READY FOR ACTION
This black panther, a black form of the leopard species, is stalking and getting ready for the kill. Every part of its body is tensed and ready for action. A cat on the prowl moves very slowly and silently until it is near enough to make a quick and decisive pounce. All cats hunt in this way, from a lion killing a buffalo, to a domestic cat killing a house mouse.

MEDIEVAL MOUSERS
This medieval picture comes from a 13th-century book called *The Harleian Bestiary*. It is interesting because it is such an early illustration of cats with a rat. For centuries, cats were suspected of being in league with witches and the devil. Despite being hunted themselves, their superb senses and agility allowed cats to survive and prosper.

IN FOR THE KILL
Cats very often choose a vantage point from which they can see but not be seen. This domestic cat would have sat absolutely silently and still on the fence for some time, watching the happenings in the grass below, before leaping down with great accuracy on the unsuspecting prey.

Black panther

A FISHY BUSINESS
The fishing cat of India does not hunt for its food quite like any other cat. It can flip fish out of the water with its slightly webbed paws, and several times has been seen diving under the surface for fish which it catches in its mouth.

TELLING TAILS
The cat's tail is a barometer of its moods. It lashes it when angry and twitches it gently to and fro when concentrating or contented.

RUNNING DOWN
The cheetah and the springboks are keeping a wary eye on each other. The cheetah will not begin to hunt unless there is a springbok on its own in a vulnerable position. The springboks know this and they will not be disturbed unless the cheetah comes too close. However, once the prey has been singled out, the cheetah will pursue it at great speed. Even so, about one or two pursuits in three are unsuccessful.

A PRACTISED KILLER
Many cats, both wild and domestic, play with their prey before killing it. Mother cats teach their kittens how to hunt by capturing prey, and releasing it, to allow the kittens to watch their actions. It is not really known why adult cats with no kittens still play with their prey. It may be that some cats need to constantly practise and hone their hunting skills.

A cat playing with a toy is reacting as if it were prey

Serval

BIG MEAL
With its massive teeth, this tiger can snap a bone with one bite, and will devour a whole carcass, skin and all.

CHICKEN DINNER
This serval of Africa, like the other small cats, crouches down to eat its food. When big cats eat, they tend to lie down with the food positioned between their front paws. Small cats begin by eating the head, which is swallowed whole with very little chewing.

COURTING COLOURS

The eastern rosella is a type of parrot from eastern Australia. In spring, the male grows splendid and colourful new feathers. He then puts on a dramatic performance to gain the attention of a female, by drooping his wings, fluffing up his breast feathers, and moving his fanned-out tail from side to side. This type of visual courtship is especially common in birds, which make much use of sight during their lives. Courting behaviour such as this is the first stage of the breeding cycle.

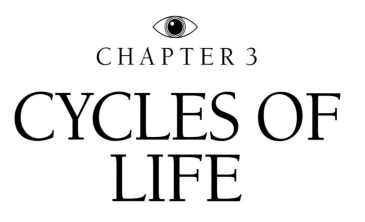

CHAPTER 3

CYCLES OF LIFE

THE ESSENTIAL HALLMARK of all living things is that they reproduce, or breed, to make more of their own kind. There are infinite ways in which animals find suitable mates, set up home, and produce and care for their young.

FIT TO BE A FATHER
Out of the breeding season, the male three-spined stickleback is a dull yellow (right, above), a handy colour for camouflage among the waterweeds. Such colours, however, hardly get him noticed in the competition to attract a female at breeding time. So he develops a deep red throat and chest, bright blue eyes, and silvery scales on his back (right, below). These colours are designed to show his health, and suitability as a father for the offspring.

Egg samples

ALL MAMMALS, including humans, are born as tiny versions of their parents. In nature, however, mammals and the way in which they give birth is unusual. Most animal mothers lay eggs. Some care for the eggs, and perhaps for the babies when they hatch. But the vast majority of animal species do not show any egg or parental care. They simply leave the eggs to hatch, protected by their tough shells. Some species bury the eggs in soft soil, or lay them in a crack or crevice for extra protection. And when these babies emerge, they must fend for themselves.

Whelk egg cases

MOLLUSC EGGS
The whelk, a type of sea snail, lays a mass of rubbery-cased eggs which it fixes to a stone. The tiny but fully formed babies crawl out of their case, and the empty egg-case bundle is often dislodged and washed up on the shore.

Egg mass under body

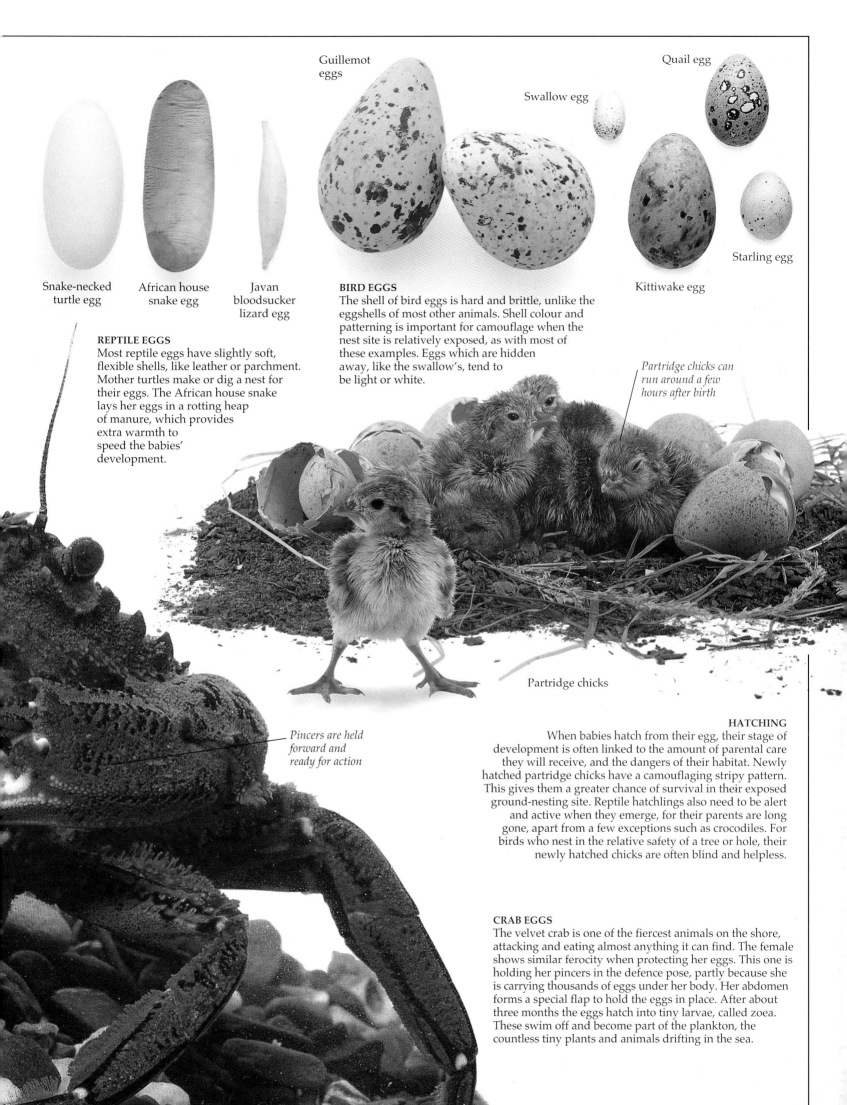

Guillemot eggs

Quail egg

Swallow egg

Snake-necked turtle egg

African house snake egg

Javan bloodsucker lizard egg

Starling egg

BIRD EGGS
The shell of bird eggs is hard and brittle, unlike the eggshells of most other animals. Shell colour and patterning is important for camouflage when the nest site is relatively exposed, as with most of these examples. Eggs which are hidden away, like the swallow's, tend to be light or white.

Kittiwake egg

REPTILE EGGS
Most reptile eggs have slightly soft, flexible shells, like leather or parchment. Mother turtles make or dig a nest for their eggs. The African house snake lays her eggs in a rotting heap of manure, which provides extra warmth to speed the babies' development.

Partridge chicks can run around a few hours after birth

Partridge chicks

Pincers are held forward and ready for action

HATCHING
When babies hatch from their egg, their stage of development is often linked to the amount of parental care they will receive, and the dangers of their habitat. Newly hatched partridge chicks have a camouflaging stripy pattern. This gives them a greater chance of survival in their exposed ground-nesting site. Reptile hatchlings also need to be alert and active when they emerge, for their parents are long gone, apart from a few exceptions such as crocodiles. For birds who nest in the relative safety of a tree or hole, their newly hatched chicks are often blind and helpless.

CRAB EGGS
The velvet crab is one of the fiercest animals on the shore, attacking and eating almost anything it can find. The female shows similar ferocity when protecting her eggs. This one is holding her pincers in the defence pose, partly because she is carrying thousands of eggs under her body. Her abdomen forms a special flap to hold the eggs in place. After about three months the eggs hatch into tiny larvae, called zoea. These swim off and become part of the plankton, the countless tiny plants and animals drifting in the sea.

Growing up

ANIMALS MAKE THE TRANSITION from baby to adult in many different ways. Some hatch or are born as miniature versions of their parents, and hardly change at all except for increasing in size. More commonly, the youngsters resemble the adults, but they differ in certain body features or proportions. Still others look nothing like their parents, as in the damselfly and other insects. Their bodies change dramatically in shape, a process called metamorphosis. As well as growing, the animal's bodily framework, be it bones on the inside (endoskeleton), or a hard casing on the outside (exoskeleton), becomes harder and tougher; its muscles develop greater strength and coordination; its sexual organs mature, ready for adulthood; and the behaviour of the creature develops as it learns to survive in the world.

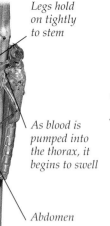

Legs hold on tightly to stem

Adult head

As blood is pumped into the thorax, it begins to swell

Abdomen

ADULT DAMSELFLY
The damselfly is a close relative of the dragonfly, but slimmer and daintier than its larger, more powerful cousin. It is just as efficient as a hunter, however, chasing gnats, midges, aphids, and other small flying insects over ponds, rivers, and waterside meadows. Unlike the dragonfly, which holds its four wings out sideways at rest, the damselfly can close its wings together over its back.

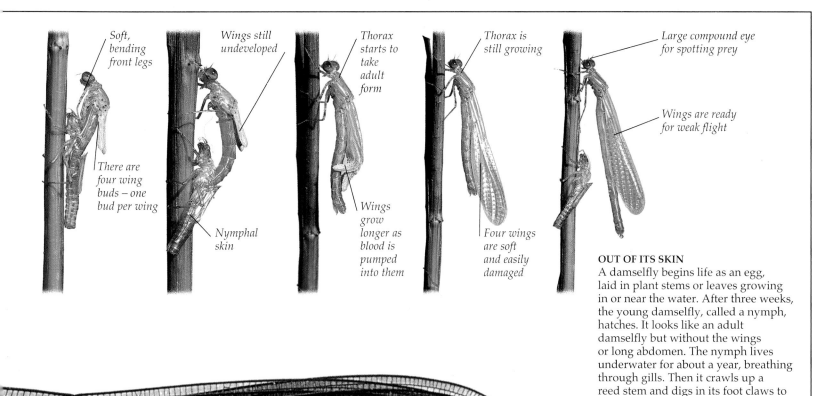

Soft, bending front legs

There are four wing buds – one bud per wing

Wings still undeveloped

Nymphal skin

Thorax starts to take adult form

Wings grow longer as blood is pumped into them

Thorax is still growing

Four wings are soft and easily damaged

Large compound eye for spotting prey

Wings are ready for weak flight

New wings are now dry and hard

OUT OF ITS SKIN

A damselfly begins life as an egg, laid in plant stems or leaves growing in or near the water. After three weeks, the young damselfly, called a nymph, hatches. It looks like an adult damselfly but without the wings or long abdomen. The nymph lives underwater for about a year, breathing through gills. Then it crawls up a reed stem and digs in its foot claws to steady itself. The skin splits along the back, and the adult damselfly pulls its head and upper body free. The crumpled wings emerge, and the adult grasps the stem above the old skin. Crawling completely free, its wings begin to expand and its abdomen lengthens. Finally its new skin and wings dry and harden. This part-change of body form during moulting is called incomplete metamorphosis.

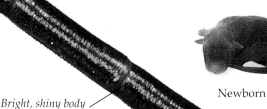

Bright, shiny body helps the damselfly to attract a mate

Abdomen is made up of many segments, so that it can bend

Male damselfly has a pair of strong claspers at the end of the abdomen. These hold on to the female during mating

Newborn   2 weeks   4 weeks   6 weeks   10 weeks

CHANGING BODIES

A typical mammal – in this case a fox – grows not only larger, but also changes its body proportions. The fox cub begins life with a large head, a snub-nosed face, a tubby body, and a short tail and legs. The short snout enables it to suck milk from its mother's teats more easily. Gradually, the nose and ears lengthen, and the face becomes more angular. The body grows faster and becomes proportionally larger. The rolls of puppy fat which kept the cub warm and provided a store of nutrients during the early weeks gradually gets used up. The cub looks much more like the adult, although it will not be fully mature for another 20–25 weeks.

Animal parents

DIFFERENT ANIMALS invest time and energy into different stages of the breeding process. Some animals produce thousands or perhaps millions of eggs, but give no later care. This is because the number of eggs is so huge, that the likelihood of one or two surviving is very great. Some animals produce only a few offspring, but these are given great care, so each has a much enhanced chance of survival. Other animals, including some fish, release millions of unprotected eggs into the water. Many other animals, including most birds and mammals from wallabies to humans, will care for their few offspring over months and even years.

FATHER FISH
The seahorse is a fish related to the perch, which shows unusual breeding behaviour. The female releases her eggs into the water, and the male gathers them into a sack-like brood pouch on his belly. The babies grow, and he "gives birth" by releasing them through a hole in the pouch.

MOTHER MARSUPIAL
The wallaby is a marsupial, or pouched animal. The baby is born tiny and very underdeveloped, as small as a child's fingertip. It crawls through its mother's fur to the pouch, or marsupium, on her underside. Here it fixes on to a teat with its mouth, and drinks milk in the usual mammal manner. Three months later it has grown large enough to leave the protection of the pouch.

Adult female red-necked wallaby

The green of the birch leaf helps to camouflage the young parent bugs

Four-month-old male red-necked wallaby

Powerful back legs ready to propel the wallaby out of danger

PARENT BUG

The parent bug is unusual among insects in that it takes great care of its young. The female lays 30-40 tiny eggs on a leaf. She then guards them for about three weeks. They hatch into tiny nymphs, very similar to herself but much smaller and without wings. The nymphs stay clustered near their mother, and their green colouring helps them to blend in with the leaf. She continues to protect them from enemies such as birds for another few weeks, until they wander off to live by themselves.

The tiny, brightly coloured nymph looks similar to the adult, except that it has no wings

Colours and scents

AMONG CRUSTACEANS, MOLLUSCS, echinoderms, and other invertebrates, relatively few species care for their eggs or offspring. But many species – insects in particular – have elaborate courtship behaviour. The striking shapes and colours of butterflies, moths, beetles, and bugs are partly to attract members of the opposite sex. They perform acrobatic courtship flights and "dances", and then feel and tap one another with their legs and antennae to assess the suitability of a potential mate. In some species, partners are attracted by airborne chemicals called pheromones.

In butterflies, it is usually the male that produces these powerful scents, while in moths it is often the female. When a male finds an interested female, they both land. The female holds her wings partly open so the male can continue spreading his scent. The mating pair may tap one another with their antennae, detecting other scents which stimulate activity at close range. Mating may last from twenty minutes to several hours, during which time the two insects remain immobile.

A 19th-century interpretation of the butterflies' courtship dance

Female lackey moth

NOT FUSSY
This caterpillar belongs to the European lackey moth. It is not a fussy eater, and will tackle the leaves of a variety of trees. The moth's eggs are on the facing page.

Sweet oil butterflies come from South America. This is the male of the mating pair

Female sweet oil butterfly

RISKY BUSINESS
Most butterflies, like this pair of sweet oil butterflies, mate on a plant. They can fly while linked together but they avoid this unless disturbed, so as not to alert the attention of hungry predators. After mating, males look for another female, but mated females seek out the food plant of their caterpillars. Although a few butterflies, notably those with grass-feeding larvae, scatter their eggs, most females actively look for a particular plant on which to lay and cement their eggs.

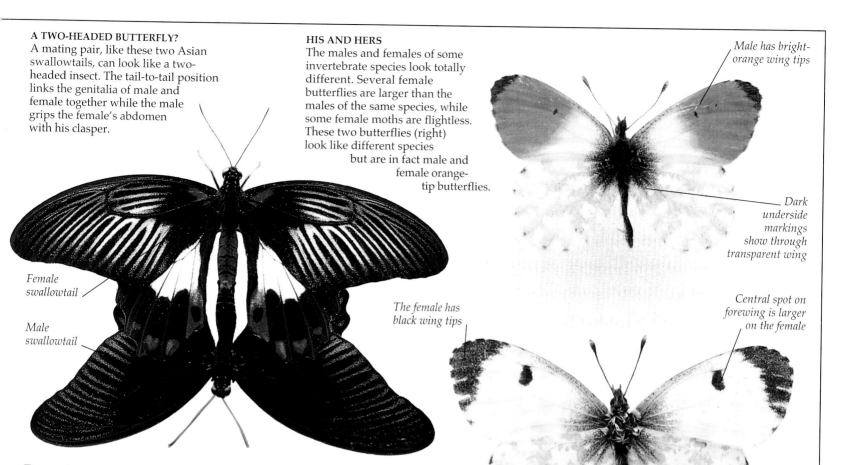

A TWO-HEADED BUTTERFLY?
A mating pair, like these two Asian
swallowtails, can look like a two-
headed insect. The tail-to-tail position
links the genitalia of male and
female together while the male
grips the female's abdomen
with his clasper.

HIS AND HERS
The males and females of some
invertebrate species look totally
different. Several female
butterflies are larger than the
males of the same species, while
some female moths are flightless.
These two butterflies (right)
look like different species
but are in fact male and
female orange-
tip butterflies.

*Male has bright-
orange wing tips*

*Dark
underside
markings
show through
transparent wing*

*The female has
black wing tips*

*Central spot on
forewing is larger
on the female*

Laying eggs

After selecting the correct plant for her
offspring to eat, the female butterfly walks over
a leaf, carefully testing to make sure it belongs
to the right plant species. Many insect species
can detect chemicals from different plants. By
putting traces of extract from cabbages on the
surface of different leaves, cabbage-eating
large and small white butterflies have even
been persuaded to lay eggs on plants that their
caterpillars will not eat.

SILK SUPPLIER
This female silkmoth has laid her batch of
eggs on a mulberry leaf. For thousands of
years, silkworms have been bred on special
silk farms, where their silk is used to weave
delicate fabrics. As a result of their domestication,
silkmoths are no longer found in the wild.

DELICATE OPERATION
This Central American Pierid
butterfly is laying her eggs on
the upper surface of the leaf.
She is very vulnerable here, as
any disturbance, such as a
heavy rainstorm, could
disrupt her task.

Some Heliconius *butterflies
lay their eggs on passion
flower tendrils*

EGG SITES
The lackey moth lays its
eggs in a ring around a twig,
so that they look like part of
the plant.

Eggs

ABOUT TO HATCH
These blue mormon butterfly eggs have
darkened and are about to hatch.
Tiny caterpillars will soon
emerge. A blue mormon
lays its eggs in a
random pattern
rather than a
cluster, so
predatory
bugs will
overlook
some of
them.

*Eggs are hidden
under leaf*

A place to breed

A goby, a common rockpool fish parent watches over its hatchlings. It will distract threats such as gulls and crabs.

THREE MAIN GROUPS of animals build special places for breeding, to shelter and protect their offspring. These are certain insects, such as wasps, bees, ants, and termites; birds, who construct all manner of nests; and mammals, who dig burrows or prepare dens. A few fish, such as sticklebacks, show parental care by building a nest for the eggs and babies. The male stickleback, shown here in his courting colours, puts great effort into fashioning a nest, impressing and luring the female there to breed, and guarding the babies as they develop. This helps to give his offspring a greater chance of survival. It is partly for this reason that sticklebacks are amongst the world's most widespread freshwater fish.

SPRING BREEDERS

Every spring, male three-spined sticklebacks develop their bright red and blue breeding colours. Spring is a good time to breed because the weather is warm and the days are long. These conditions encourage the growth of plants, on which all animal life depends. The male stakes out his own patch of water, called a territory, where he can set up his nest and chase away rival males.

Piece of water plant in stickleback's mouth for the nest

Bright – blue eye

Red throat

1 COLLECTING THE MATERIALS
The male stickleback sets about collecting little bits of water plants for the nest.

Beneath a small boulder is the ideal site on which to build a nest

Stickleback shovels gravel with his snout

2 DIGGING THE FOUNDATION
He pushes his snout into the stones and mud of the bottom, shovelling them aside to make a shallow hole. The nest is often found among water weeds or in the shelter of a small rock.

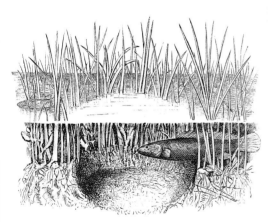

MULTI-FAMILY FATHER
The male bowfin, a fish from eastern North America, has several breeding partners. Each spring he makes a rough scoop of gravel, roots, and other plant pieces, usually in a swampy part of his lake or river home. One or more females lay the eggs, which the male fertilizes and then guards until the larvae hatch. These stick themselves into the nest by glue glands on their heads, feeding off the food reserves called yolk in their eggs, until they can swim freely.

3 A FIRM BASE
As the male begins to push plant pieces into place, he taps and prods them firmly to make a secure base. The large fan-like pectoral fins are useful for the precise manoeuvring that this process requires.

Stickleback makes a firm base by prodding weeds into place with his snout

4 CEMENT STAGE
As the pile of nest material grows, the male cements it together with a sticky "glue", a secretion made by specialized parts of his kidneys. Gradually the nest grows, layer by layer.

Dogfish egg cases

Fan-like pectoral fins create a current of water to aerate the nest

INDIVIDUAL PROTECTION
Instead of a communal nest and a guardian parent like the stickleback, the female dogfish gives each of her babies its own leathery suit for protection. She lays her egg cases in pairs, attached to seaweed by long, curly tendrils at each corner. The embryos grow inside, living on the stored food, or yolk. After 6 to 9 months the young dogfish wriggle out at around 10 cm (4 in) long. The empty egg cases are often washed up on the beach as "mermaid's purses".

5 ADDED VENTILATION
The collection of weeds and glue prevents a good flow of fresh water through the nest, which will be needed to keep the eggs well aerated. So the fish uses his large fins to fan a current of water through the nest.

Mouth agape in "yawn"

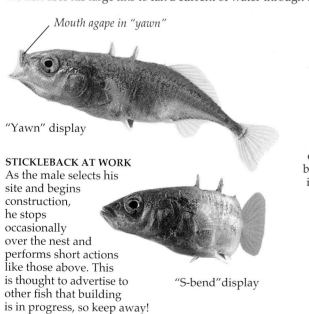

"Yawn" display

STICKLEBACK AT WORK
As the male selects his site and begins construction, he stops occasionally over the nest and performs short actions like those above. This is thought to advertise to other fish that building is in progress, so keep away!

"S-bend" display

COMPLICATED COURTING
Baby animals develop from the mother's eggs, which are fertilized by father's sperm. On land, the male and female usually get close together to transfer sperm. In water, many creatures simply release their eggs and sperm into the water, and trust to chance. The dragonet, a fish from Europe, improves on this method. The female lies under the colourful male. They form a channel with their anal fins into which the sperm and eggs are shed and mixed, before wafting away into the water.

Male and female dragonet pair, ready to release eggs and sperm

Courtship spectacular

Raggiana bird of paradise

O F ALL THE VERTEBRATE ANIMALS, the most spectacular courtship ceremonies are performed by birds. In many species, the male is the star performer. He flies, dances, sings, shakes his shimmering plumage, and perhaps inflates a balloon-like pouch of skin to attract one or more females. After mating, the female will usually carry out egg-sitting and chick-feeding duties: she usually has dull feathers, to camouflage her on the nest. In birds who share the family-rearing duties more equally, plumage colours and patterns vary less between male and female. Almost every conceivable partnership arrangement exists somewhere in the bird world. Some species attract a single mate and remain faithful to her for life, while other species use their brilliant courtship plumage to attract a whole series of mates, deserting each one for the next as soon as mating has taken place.

ROLE REVERSAL
Unusually for a bird, the female red phalarope courts the male. She is the more brightly coloured of the two birds.

THE PEACOCK'S TAIL
Peacocks are members of the pheasant family, a group of birds which show some of the most spectacular and elaborate courtship plumage in the bird world.

HIDDEN SUPPORT
From the back, the upright feathers of the peacock's "true tail" can be seen. These brace the much longer and more brilliant tail coverts.

ON PARADE
Male lyrebirds make themselves arenas in the hilly forests of eastern Australia, on which they strut and display. Their posturing attracts a succession of mates. The female builds a large nest and cares for the babies.

Feathers without barbules do not interlock, so appear lacy

A MYSTERY SOLVED

It was only in the last century that naturalists penetrated the forests of New Guinea and saw the Raggiana bird of paradise using its plumage. During courtship displays, the male bird hangs upside down and throws its plumes open.

Body feathers

Streaked central feather

Hair-like golden plumes

Softer display feathers towards edge

During display, feathers open to produce a fountain of colour as the male bird swings upside down from a branch

Many birds moult their colourful breeding feathers after mating is over and grow duller ones for camouflage during the rest of the year

INFLATABLE ATTRACTION

The male frigate bird has a brilliant red throat pouch which he uses to attract a mate. He keeps his pouch inflated for many hours until a female, lured by his irresistible courtship device, joins him.

DEFUSING TENSION

Boobies and gannets nest in densely packed colonies, stabbing any neighbour which dares to intrude on another's private patch. A lengthy courtship is needed between pairs to defuse this aggression. Here, two blue-footed boobies join in the "pelican" display, pointing their beaks out of each other's way.

IN STEP WITH THE SEASON

The brilliant colours on puffins' beaks are at their brightest during the breeding season in early summer. The colour lies in a horny sheath that covers the outside of the beak. When the puffins abandon their cliff-top burrows and head out to sea for the winter, this sheath falls off. The beak is then a much more subdued colour until the following spring.

DANCING IN WATER

Great crested grebes perform bizarre dances during their courtship. They often begin with a head-shaking dance, in which the birds face each other, jerking their heads from side to side. Suddenly, they dive and reappear at the surface with beakfuls of waterweed. During the "penguin dance" both birds rear up out of the water, paddling furiously as they present the weed to each other. After several more set-pieces, the birds mate.

MINIATURE RIVALS

A territory in which to nest and collect food is a necessity for successful pairing in many bird species. These male hummingbirds, though tiny, are pugnaciously defending their territories.

Common European Oyster

Slow and steady shells

UNLIKE THE STOP-GO GROWTH of insects and crustaceans, or the drastic change in body shape shown by amphibians, the growth of molluscs is relatively steady and slow. By depositing crystals of calcium carbonate on a framework of protein, called conchiolin, a hard shell is created so that the soft creature is always protected. The part of the mollusc that makes these secretions is a sheet of soft tissue called the mantle, which is located between the shell itself and the inner organs. Around the lip of a live mollusc's shell is a thin, flexible layer of developing shelly matter – it is at this point that a shell is most vulnerable and many molluscs have therefore developed a trap door, called an operculum, to protect the exposed part of the body. Some molluscs have periods of fast and then slow growth, creating a shell of varying thicknesses. These growth marks, or rings, are very evident in some shells, such as oysters.

OYSTER GROWTH RINGS
Oysters develop from minute eggs, only 2 mm (0.08 in) long, that settle onto a hard substrate after about two weeks of drifting, and begin to develop a shell. Many oysters have characteristic growth rings on their top valves, like those that can be seen when a tree trunk is sliced through.

BREAKING AWAY
The early, more fragile whorls do not contain living tissues and are often broken off or eroded over the years.

Tortoise shell

A LIVING JIGSAW
As tortoises and turtles grow older, their horny plates and bony shields fit together like a living jigsaw.

FADING FAST
As the shell ages, the once brightly coloured juvenile whorls start to fade.

Triton shell

GROWING UP GRADUALLY
As with many molluscs, the triton develops from a microscopic larva, known as a veliger. After varying degrees of time, the larva settles to develop a shell – in some tritons, this can take a year. As with the oyster, there are distinct growth marks, though here the growth stages are characterized by a thickening of the lip at each stage and, in the adult shell, these can be seen as pronounced ridges.

Adult coloration and ridging begin to appear

Juvenile shell

Young shell has a fine lip

At each new whorl of the spiral, the mollusc pauses to thicken its aperture

AT HOME WITH A HERMIT

Most crabs are totally protected by a hard outer exoskeleton, which they shed at intervals to grow. But the hermit crab has a relatively soft body and adopts an old mollusc shell as a portable protective shelter. As it grows, the crab discards its shell and goes in search of a bigger home.

Crab secures itself inside shells with this hook

Great hermit crab inside an old Neapolitan triton shell

Juvenile whorls now faded and eroded

OLD AGE

When a mollusc reaches old age, it does not add new whorls but will continue to lay down calcium salts, therefore thickening its existing shell.

The characteristic lip thickenings of earlier growth stages are called varices

Central column inside shell is called the columella

Older shell material becomes more brittle and flaky

As the whorls get larger, the spiral ridges become more pronounced

NEARLY THERE

The almost adult shell is poised to develop its characteristic teeth and colouring within the aperture.

Fully developed shell is thick and heavy, and its coloration is strong

Wide aperture with teeth on the lip

Eggs and hatching

APART FROM THE AMPHIBIANS, most vertebrate animals are born or hatch as smaller versions of their parents. All birds and many reptiles hatch from tough-shelled eggs, although some mother snakes and lizards give birth to fully formed babies rather than laying eggs. All mammals except the platypus and echidna also give birth. The new babies then grow steadily by getting bigger all over, rather than changing their body shape or form. As the new babies enlarge, they alter their feeding habits according to the type and size of food items they can deal with. A young crocodile, for example, may be able to survive on insects, but, as it grows bigger, it will eat considerably larger prey, including mammals, birds, and fish.

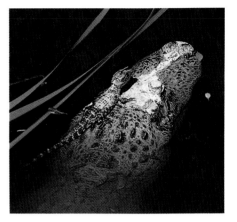

Young caiman

LIKE MOTHER LIKE DAUGHTER
This young caiman meets the world fully formed and able to fend for itself. Like the young alligator, it will stay close to its mother for a few weeks, sometimes using her back as a basking platform. Despite the mother's care, unusual in reptiles, at the first sign of danger the young are able to dive under water for cover.

HATCHING OUT
Once they are laid, snake eggs often swell and get heavier as they absorb moisture from the surroundings, but the length of time needed before they hatch varies according to the temperature. The warmer it is, the faster the eggs develop, so the parent often chooses to lay them in a place that is both warm and slightly moist. Piles of vegetation produce heat as the plant material rots, so compost heaps are sometimes selected as nesting sites, particularly by snakes living in cooler areas. The hatchling is often much longer than the egg from which it hatched. This is possible because, as the embryo develops, the whole body is coiled into a tight spiral.

1 THE EGG
This is the egg of a rat snake, a common and rather large snake from North America. Its mating season is from April to June and also in the autumn. Between June and August the female lays 5 to 30 soft-shelled, oblong eggs, often choosing rotten wood, leaf litter, or a spot under some rocks as her "nest".

4 MAKING A MOVE
The snake leaves the egg quite quickly. It is able to slither along in the normal snake-like way immediately. Interestingly, however, if a snake is removed from its egg a little too early, it will writhe about, unable to move along properly, although in every other way it looks quite normal. It therefore seems likely that the snake only becomes fully co-ordinated just before hatching.

BORN, THEN "HATCHED"
Baby adders develop inside their mother's body. They are born inside thin egg membranes, from which they soon struggle free.

LOOKS CAN DECEIVE
Most geckos lay their eggs between pieces of bark or stuck to a wall. This sandstone gecko laid her eggs between the crevices of rocks, and because they were exposed to the elements, they had hard shells. Many lizards, snakes, and turtles have leathery-shelled eggs, while in tortoises and crocodiles the shell is harder and more brittle. Although many geckos lay their eggs in shared sites, they take no care of their young at all – in fact, it is unusual that mother and young should be as close to one another as this.

Female

Young

THE HAZARDS OF HATCHING
Among the reptiles, turtles lay the most eggs, but care for them the least. Abandoned to the earth or sand in which its egg was buried, from the start this little hatchling will have to fight alone to survive in a dangerous world.

The young snake checks its surroundings with its tongue

Slit made by egg tooth

The snake is in no hurry to leave the safety of its shell

2 BREAKING THE SHELL
While it is developing inside the egg, the young rat snake takes nourishment from the yolk. A day or two before hatching, the yolk sac is drawn into the body and the remaining yolk is absorbed into the young snake's intestine. A small scar, rather like a navel, shows the point where the embryo was joined to its food supply. As the young snake develops, a sharp, but temporary "egg tooth" grows from the tip of its upper jaw and the hatchling uses this to pierce the egg shell. The young snake gets its first view of the world through one of the slits it makes.

3 LEAVING THE EGG
Having tested its surroundings by flicking its tongue in and out to "taste" the air, the young snake cautiously peers from its shell. It will be in no hurry to leave, and may stay where it is, with only its head poking out, for a day or two. That way, if disturbed, it can always go back inside the egg. Rat snakes can be ready to leave their eggs any time between 7–15 weeks after laying.

Adult colour and pattern is already developed on scales

5 MINOR MIRACLE
Fully out of its shell now, it seems amazing that such a long snake could ever have been packed inside such a relatively small egg. The hatchlings may be as much as seven times longer than the egg, at 28-40 cm (11–16 in) in length.

Caring parents

TWO GROUPS OF ANIMALS develop and grow in a most remarkable way. These are the amphibians and the insects, and the life cycle feature they have in common is metamorphosis – change in body shape. In amphibians this happens as eggs hatch into tadpoles, which change into adults. Most amphibians return to water or a damp place to breed. The female lays her soft, jelly-covered eggs, or spawn, and the male fertilizes them with his sperm. In many species, the eggs are then left as the parents disperse. But some amphibians are dutiful parents and take care of their eggs and offspring. The kind of care ranges from choosing a sheltered egglaying site, to enclosing eggs in a protective foam, to guarding the eggs. Some amphibians carry their eggs or tadpoles on their back, or in a skin pocket; others take their eggs inside the body, into vocal sacs, or even into the stomach.

STOMACH UPSET
This fairy tale character looks as though she is having a bad time. So are the most remarkable frogs of all – the Australian gastric brooding frogs, first discovered in 1972. The female swallows her eggs, and the tadpoles develop into tiny froglets in her stomach.

SAFETY DEPOSIT BOX
The back of this female marsupial, or pouched, frog from South America looks swollen. After she laid a hundred or more fertilized eggs, the male placed them in the brood pouch on her back. After incubation, the female makes her way to the water. Using the toes on her back feet, she then opens up the pouch, releasing the tadpoles into the water to complete their development.

EGG MIMIC
The patterns on the back of these two glass frogs from the rainforests of Costa Rica look very similar to the eggs they are guarding. The male's camouflage enables him to guard the eggs in safety for 24 hours a day. As these frogs are so well camouflaged, they can avoid predators and feed on any insects that may alight on the leaf.

A LONG WAIT
This little lungless salamander, found in Costa Rica and Panama, is a devoted parent, guarding its egg clutch for some four to five months. The guarding parent, which may be either the male or the female, lies curled around the eggs, which it turns occasionally. This protects the eggs from both predators and fungal infection.

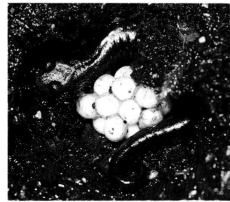

Male midwife toad, ranging from 3–5 cm (1.25–2 in) in length, carries a string of eggs

A SAFE PLACE

The female Surinam toad from South America looks like dead leaves on the muddy bottom of the sluggish waters in which it lives. After mating, the male fertilizes the eggs released by the female, which stick on to a thick, spongy layer of skin on her back.

Skin of female Surinam toad swells up, almost covering her eggs

Some males take on two, or even three, egg clutches

POCKETS FULL OF TOADLETS

The eggs are placed on the female Surinam toad's back when the male and female perform an egglaying roll, or loop movement, underwater. The pair are upside down when the female lays about five eggs which are fertilized and drop on to her back as the pair turn right way up in the water. In all, about 55 eggs are laid in this way. After four weeks they hatch as perfect, small toadlets.

HITCHING A LIFT

This little non-poisonous frog from Trinidad is related to the more brightly coloured poison-dart frogs from Central and South America. In this species, the male stays with its egg clutch. When they hatch, he carries the entire tadpole brood on his back to a nearby stream to complete their development. In other closely related species, the female is the tadpole carrier.

VOCAL SAC BROODING

The male Darwin's frog from Chile watches over his developing clutch of eggs. When the newly hatched tadpoles start to squirm, he takes them into his vocal sac, or "chin". The tadpoles remain there, apparently receiving some form of nourishment, until they are ejected as tiny froglets.

THE MALE MIDWIFE

The male midwife toad from western Europe shows a unique form of parental care – he carries his eggstring of some 35–50 eggs, wrapped around his hind legs. After the eggs are laid and fertilized, he keeps hold of the female and, moving his legs alternately back and forth through the eggs, fastens them securely around his legs. After about three weeks, he takes his egg load into the water where the tadpoles hatch and complete their development.

Tadpole to frog

NOW A FROGLET
At 12 weeks, the tail has reduced to a stump and will soon disappear. The froglets are ready to leave the water. Every generation re-enacts the transition from water to land that occurred in the first amphibians.

METAMORPHOSIS IS the change in body shape as an animal grows from an immature larval form to its mature adult form. Amphibians are the only land vertebrates to develop in this way. Frog and toad larvae, or tadpoles, look completely different from their parents. The most notable difference is that a tadpole has an all-in-one head and body, as well as a long tail.

At first a tadpole lacks legs, which develop later, and it must live in water to survive. The time taken to develop from eggs hatching to a fully formed froglet varies from about 12 to 16 weeks, but this time span is greatly affected by water temperature and food supply. Tadpoles found in colder regions, at high altitudes, or from spawn laid in the breeding season, may hibernate in the tadpole state, and will not turn into a frog until the following spring. This is the life cycle of the common or European frog, from a tadpole with gills, tail, and no legs, to an adult with lungs, legs, and no tail.

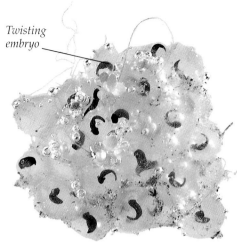

Twisting embryo

2 LIFE BEGINS
After fertilization, the single egg cell in the dark blob of yolk divides into two, then four, then eight, and so on. Gradually the developing embryo grows longer and takes on a comma shape, still enclosed in its protective jelly. It becomes a tadpole and hatches about six days after fertilization.

Frog's egg

Female common frog

A pair of common frogs in amplexus

Male common frog

1 A TIGHT SQUEEZE
The male frog is clasping the female underneath him, in a tight, mating embrace, called "amplexus". The male grasps the female behind her front legs – in other species, the grasp may be in front of her hind legs or around her head. Amplexus can last for several days. The male fertilizes the eggs, which in this species number about 2,000. In other species the eggs can vary from one up to 20,000, or more. They may be laid singly, in clumps, or in strings.

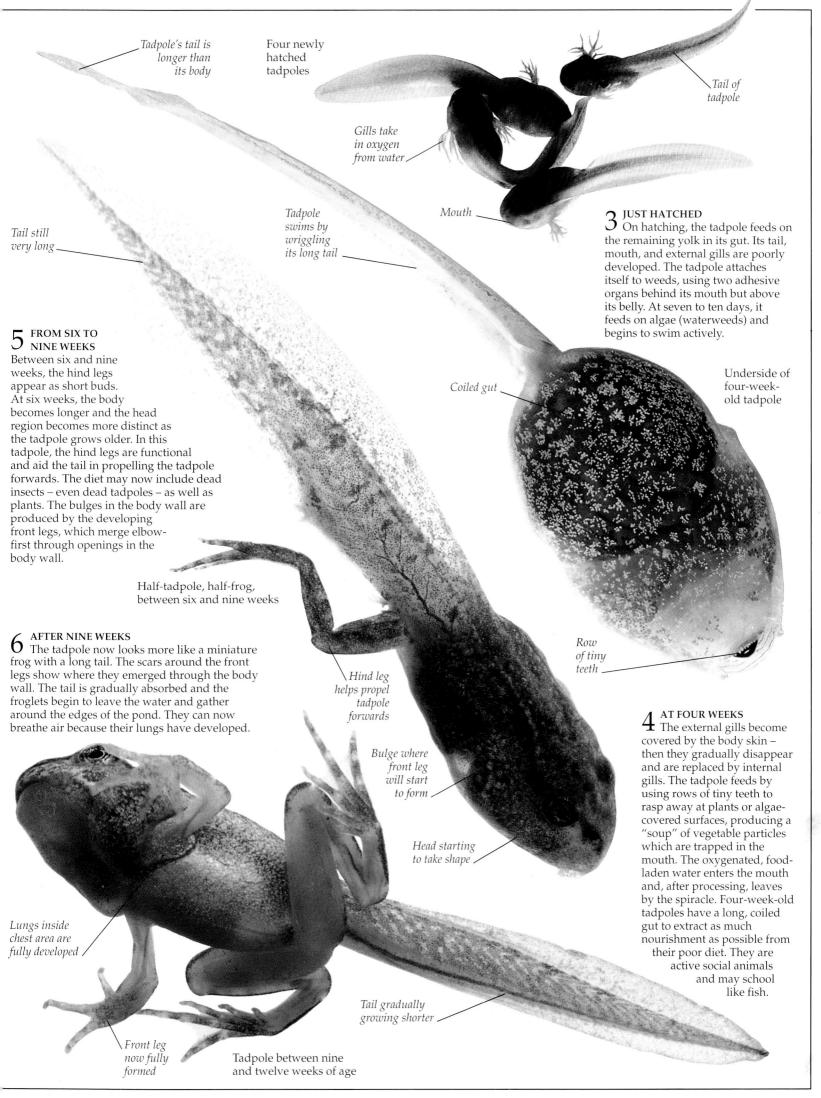

Tadpole's tail is
longer than
its body

Four newly
hatched tadpoles

Tail of
tadpole

Gills take
in oxygen
from water

Mouth

Tadpole
swims by
wriggling
its long tail

Tail still
very long

3 JUST HATCHED
On hatching, the tadpole feeds on
the remaining yolk in its gut. Its tail,
mouth, and external gills are poorly
developed. The tadpole attaches
itself to weeds, using two adhesive
organs behind its mouth but above
its belly. At seven to ten days, it
feeds on algae (waterweeds) and
begins to swim actively.

Coiled gut

Underside of
four-week-
old tadpole

5 FROM SIX TO NINE WEEKS
Between six and nine
weeks, the hind legs
appear as short buds.
At six weeks, the body
becomes longer and the head
region becomes more distinct as
the tadpole grows older. In this
tadpole, the hind legs are functional
and aid the tail in propelling the tadpole
forwards. The diet may now include dead
insects – even dead tadpoles – as well as
plants. The bulges in the body wall are
produced by the developing
front legs, which merge elbow-
first through openings in the
body wall.

Half-tadpole, half-frog,
between six and nine weeks

6 AFTER NINE WEEKS
The tadpole now looks more like a miniature
frog with a long tail. The scars around the front
legs show where they emerged through the body
wall. The tail is gradually absorbed and the
froglets begin to leave the water and gather
around the edges of the pond. They can now
breathe air because their lungs have developed.

Row
of tiny
teeth

Hind leg
helps propel
tadpole
forwards

Bulge where
front leg
will start
to form

Head starting
to take shape

4 AT FOUR WEEKS
The external gills become
covered by the body skin –
then they gradually disappear
and are replaced by internal
gills. The tadpole feeds by
using rows of tiny teeth to
rasp away at plants or algae-
covered surfaces, producing a
"soup" of vegetable particles
which are trapped in the
mouth. The oxygenated, food-
laden water enters the mouth
and, after processing, leaves
by the spiracle. Four-week-old
tadpoles have a long, coiled
gut to extract as much
nourishment as possible from
their poor diet. They are
active social animals
and may school
like fish.

Lungs inside
chest area are
fully developed

Tail gradually
growing shorter

Front leg
now fully
formed

Tadpole between nine
and twelve weeks of age

Caterpillar to chrysalis

THE CATERPILLAR is often regarded as simply the feeding stage in the life cycle of a butterfly, but it is a complex animal in its own right. It has to be capable of surviving in a hostile world, and it has to prepare for the vital transformation to the next, immobile stage, the chrysalis. Insects have two different kinds of metamorphosis. In grasshoppers, crickets, bugs, dragonflies, cockroaches and others, there is a slight change each time the insect moults and changes its skin. This is incomplete metamorphosis. In butterflies, moths, ants, bees, wasps, and beetles, there is a much more dramatic all-in-one change at certain stages during life. This is complete metamorphosis. The following pages show the life cycle of a butterfly from pupa or chrysalis, to imago or adult.

False legs or prolegs

HANGING AROUND
Some caterpillars and chrysalises hang straight down without the support of a silken girdle. The skin splits along the caterpillar's back to reveal the chrysalis.

Some species use their silk thread to bind together leaves for protection

1 FINDING A SITE
The caterpillar of the citrus swallowtail butterfly selects a suitable site to turn into a pupa. Its hind claspers grip the plant stem.

The caterpillar is held in place by a strong silken girdle

LEAF ROLLERS
For added safety, some species pupate inside a rolled-up leaf. If disturbed on the leaf, the caterpillar will drop down on a silken thread and climb back up on to the leaf when danger has passed.

Immobile pupa resembles dead leaf

New chrysalis skin

Empty skin and legs of caterpillar

5 SPLITTING AT THE SEAMS
The caterpillar wriggles vigorously and its skin starts to split along its back. The new chrysalis skin beneath is beginning to show through.

Skin is starting to split

6 NEW SKIN FOR OLD
The caterpillar's movements gradually force off its old skin. The chrysalis skin starts to harden as it is exposed to the air.

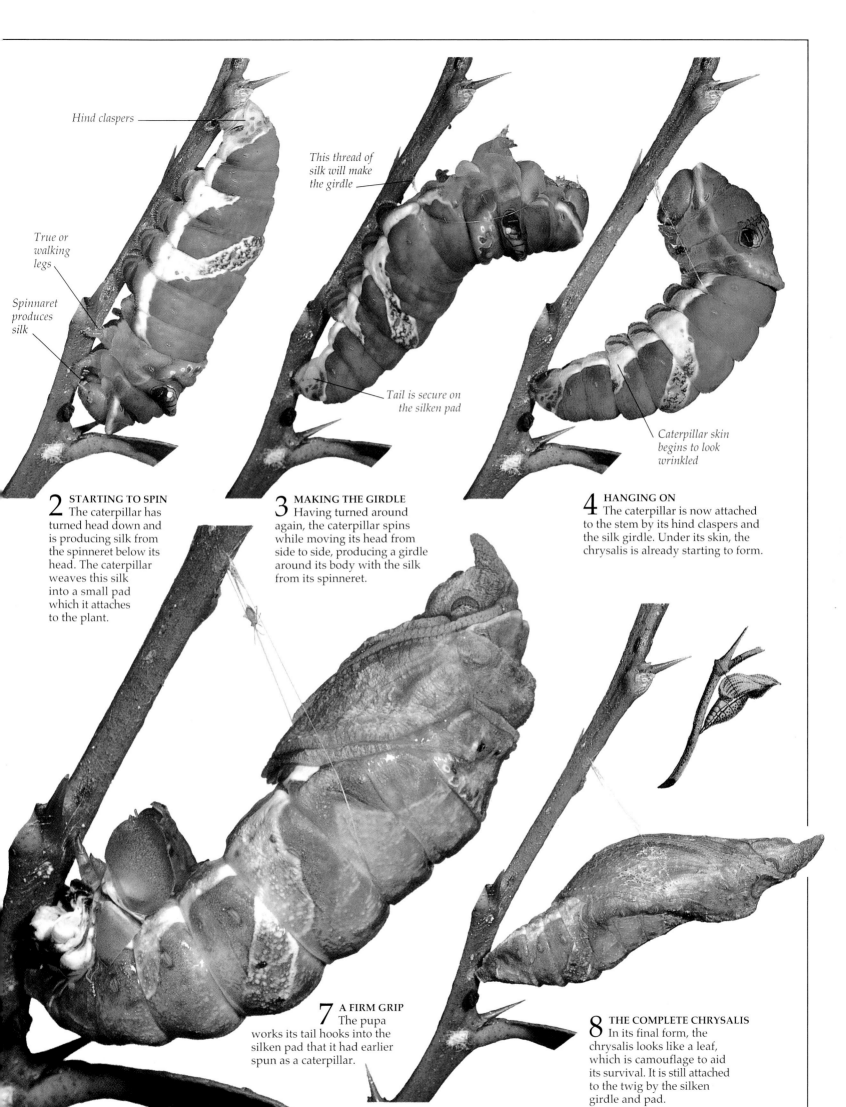

Hind claspers

This thread of
silk will make
the girdle

True or
walking
legs

Spinnaret
produces
silk

Tail is secure on
the silken pad

Caterpillar skin
begins to look
wrinkled

2 STARTING TO SPIN
The caterpillar has turned head down and is producing silk from the spinneret below its head. The caterpillar weaves this silk into a small pad which it attaches to the plant.

3 MAKING THE GIRDLE
Having turned around again, the caterpillar spins while moving its head from side to side, producing a girdle around its body with the silk from its spinneret.

4 HANGING ON
The caterpillar is now attached to the stem by its hind claspers and the silk girdle. Under its skin, the chrysalis is already starting to form.

7 A FIRM GRIP
The pupa works its tail hooks into the silken pad that it had earlier spun as a caterpillar.

8 THE COMPLETE CHRYSALIS
In its final form, the chrysalis looks like a leaf, which is camouflage to aid its survival. It is still attached to the twig by the silken girdle and pad.

Chrysalis to butterfly

A BUTTERFLY CHRYSALIS, or pupa, may hang quite still for several weeks or, in some species, right through the winter. Nothing seems to happen but, within the hard case, tremendous changes are taking place. The body tissues are completely broken down, and reassembled into the adult butterfly with antennae, wings, and other delicate features. Across these pages, you can see a blue morpho from Central and South America emerging from its pupal case.

"THE FLIGHT FROM EGYPT"
A blue morpho butterfly is used in the border around this illustration from *Hastings Hours*, an illuminated manuscript from c.1480.

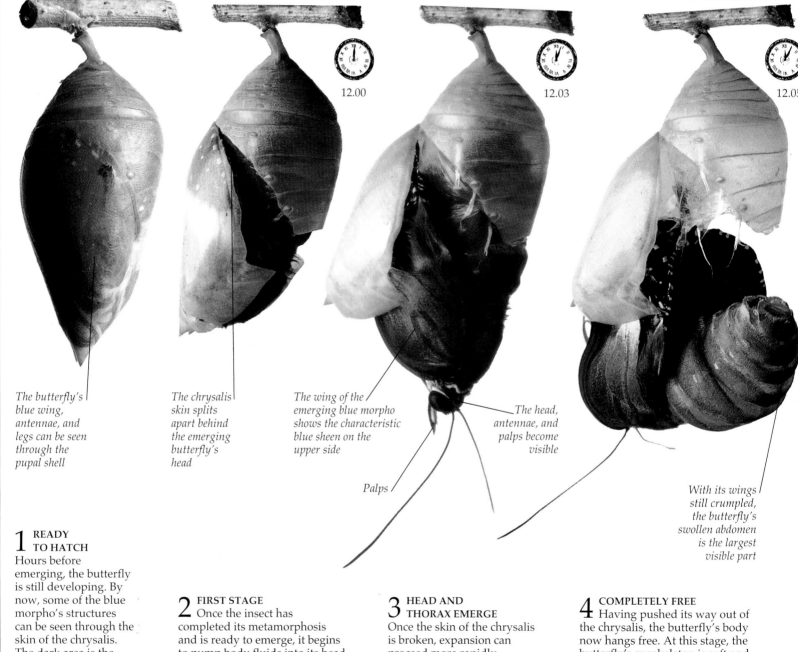

12.00

12.03

12.05

The butterfly's blue wing, antennae, and legs can be seen through the pupal shell

The chrysalis skin splits apart behind the emerging butterfly's head

The wing of the emerging blue morpho shows the characteristic blue sheen on the upper side

The head, antennae, and palps become visible

Palps

With its wings still crumpled, the butterfly's swollen abdomen is the largest visible part

1 READY TO HATCH
Hours before emerging, the butterfly is still developing. By now, some of the blue morpho's structures can be seen through the skin of the chrysalis. The dark area is the butterfly's wing, and traces of the antennae and legs are visible toward the bottom of the chrysalis. It takes about 85 days after the egg is laid for a blue morpho adult to emerge.

2 FIRST STAGE
Once the insect has completed its metamorphosis and is ready to emerge, it begins to pump body fluids into its head and thorax. This helps to split the chrysalis along certain weak points, so that the adult insect can begin to force its way out.

3 HEAD AND THORAX EMERGE
Once the skin of the chrysalis is broken, expansion can proceed more rapidly. Inflation is due not only to the body fluids in the head and thorax, but also to the air the insect takes in. Although by now the antennae, head, and palps (smaller tasting mouthparts) are visible, the wings are still too soft and crumpled for proper identification.

4 COMPLETELY FREE
Having pushed its way out of the chrysalis, the butterfly's body now hangs free. At this stage, the butterfly's exoskeleton is soft and still capable of more expansion. If for any reason the butterfly is damaged at this stage or confined, perhaps by a thoughtless collector, complete expansion is not possible. All the parts harden and a crippled butterfly results.

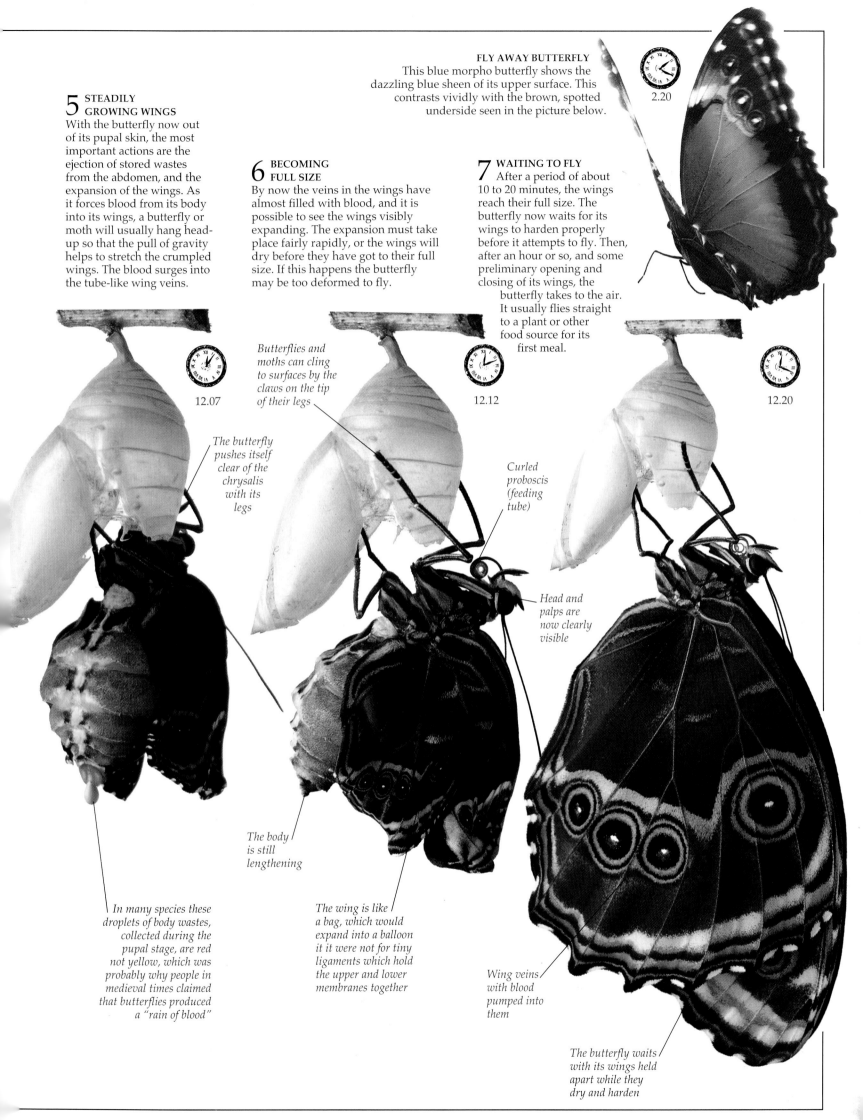

5 STEADILY GROWING WINGS

With the butterfly now out of its pupal skin, the most important actions are the ejection of stored wastes from the abdomen, and the expansion of the wings. As it forces blood from its body into its wings, a butterfly or moth will usually hang head-up so that the pull of gravity helps to stretch the crumpled wings. The blood surges into the tube-like wing veins.

6 BECOMING FULL SIZE

By now the veins in the wings have almost filled with blood, and it is possible to see the wings visibly expanding. The expansion must take place fairly rapidly, or the wings will dry before they have got to their full size. If this happens the butterfly may be too deformed to fly.

7 WAITING TO FLY

After a period of about 10 to 20 minutes, the wings reach their full size. The butterfly now waits for its wings to harden properly before it attempts to fly. Then, after an hour or so, and some preliminary opening and closing of its wings, the butterfly takes to the air. It usually flies straight to a plant or other food source for its first meal.

FLY AWAY BUTTERFLY
This blue morpho butterfly shows the dazzling blue sheen of its upper surface. This contrasts vividly with the brown, spotted underside seen in the picture below.

2.20

12.07

Butterflies and moths can cling to surfaces by the claws on the tip of their legs

The butterfly pushes itself clear of the chrysalis with its legs

In many species these droplets of body wastes, collected during the pupal stage, are red not yellow, which was probably why people in medieval times claimed that butterflies produced a "rain of blood"

12.12

The body is still lengthening

The wing is like a bag, which would expand into a balloon it it were not for tiny ligaments which hold the upper and lower membranes together

Curled proboscis (feeding tube)

Head and palps are now clearly visible

12.20

Wing veins with blood pumped into them

The butterfly waits with its wings held apart while they dry and harden

Hatched at an early age

Birds and mammals, with their relatively large brains and adaptable behaviour, are the two groups of animals which provide most parental care. Birds who nest on the ground or in exposed places tend to have chicks that hatch in a well-developed state, with strong legs, eyes open, and feathers partly grown, ready to run from predators. However, the newly hatched young of the more protected tree and hole-nesters are at a much more immature stage, with bare skin, wing and leg stumps, and naked skin. But they develop almost before your eyes, as shown by these blue tit babies and their tireless parents.

Feeding the children

Wing

Leg

Mouth is brightly coloured to attract attention

Feather tufts

Jointed eyelids

Feather tract

Feather sheaths

1 ONE DAY OLD
Twenty-four hours after hatching, blue tit nestlings have no feathers and their eyes are closed. During the day, both parents leave the nestlings to search for food. However, the young never remain on their own for long, because their parents return to the nest with food every few minutes. The parents may make up to 1,000 return journeys between them per day.

BIRD OF GOOD OMEN
Faithful to its mate and tireless as a parent, the stork is recognized internationally as a symbol of the birth of a new human baby.

2 THREE DAYS OLD
In a scene all too familiar to their weary parents, the growing nestlings beg for food. Their instinctive reaction is triggered off by their parents' arrival at the nest, or sometimes by the parents' calls. By the third day, small tufts of feathers have appeared, and the nestlings are about four times heavier than when they hatched.

3 FIVE DAYS OLD
By this time, dark grey feather tracts have appeared down the nestlings' backs and on their wings. These are areas of skin which are destined to produce the feathers. On the wings, the tubular sheaths which will eventually produce and protect the flight feathers have already started to develop.

Feather sheaths

Emerging feather tips

ESCAPE FROM DANGER

Although most birds protect their nestlings by bluff or aggression when threatened, some parents can pick up their young and carry them away. Depending on the species, they may use either their beak, legs, or talons.

The woodcock is said to hold a chick between its legs while flying, although this has never been proved

The secretive water rail carries its chicks in its long beak

Hawks are thought to hold their nestlings in their talons as they carry them to a safer place

4 NINE DAYS OLD

As the feather sheaths grow longer, the tips of the flight feathers start to emerge. The bare skin between the feather tracts is covered up by the growing feathers. The nest is starting to get crowded, although for blue tits, five nestlings is quite a small family.

5 THIRTEEN DAYS OLD

At nearly two weeks, the nestlings are fully fledged and their eyes are open. Within another five days they will leave the nest, but the young birds will follow their parents for some time, begging for food as they learn how to look after themselves. Independence often comes when the parents begin preparations for another clutch of eggs. Once the young birds find that their parents are ignoring their calls for food, they fend for themselves.

Unique to mammals

MARE AND FOAL
A mare nudges her foal towards her two teats; the foal then feeds on average some 4 times each hour

THE MAMMAL GROUP is named after the mammary glands – body parts that produce nourishing milk to feed a newborn baby. Milk is the young mammal's complete food, providing even the water it needs. No other animal possesses mammary glands, so no other mother can feed her offspring on milk. The actual glands resemble specialized sweat glands and grow into two "milk lines" on each side of the abdomen. Cats and dogs have several glands and teats along each side; in hoofed animals they are near the hind legs. In monkeys, apes, and humans, they are on the chest, a site that may be connected with adaptation to a tree-dwelling life and the consequent need to hold a baby with the forelimbs. Another body part unique to female womb. The baby develops inside this, kept warm, protected, and nourished, until ready for birth.

Mother watches and listens in case of danger

The mother lies still as her babies feed

THE NEAT TEAT
Unlike kittens, puppies usually feed from whichever teat they can find. The teat (or nipple) is a rubbery-textured lobe of tissue. It fits neatly inside the baby's mouth, to minimize loss of milk as the baby suckles. The teat also acts as a shut-off valve to prevent leakage of milk after feeding.

CONTENTED CAT AND KITTENS
Within an hour of birth, a kitten is suckling (sucking milk from its mother's teat). Since there is usually about 30 minutes between the births of successive offspring in a litter, and there are four or five kittens in an average litter, the first-born will already be suckling when the later ones arrive. The tiny kitten, although unable to see or hear, can smell – and can feel with its whiskers, fur, nose, and feet. It moves to the milk supply by scrabbling with its feet, first locating the warmth of the mother's body, then working its way along until it finds a teat. It "kneads" the teat with its feet and face to stimulate the milk flow. After an initial free-for-all, each kitten tends to settle into a routine and suckle from its own teat. In a large litter, the young may feed in shifts.

Teats run along the length of the mother's abdomen

The litter is small, so this teat is not needed by any kitten

MATERNAL MANATEE
The manatee, a marine mammal, has teats situated just behind her front flippers, near her "armpits". The youngster feeds underwater, lying by its mother's side in calm water. Sometimes the mother holds the baby with her flipper to prevent it floating about in water currents, a bit like a human mother cradling her infant.

Each kitten has its own teat

Newborn kittens feeding on their mother's milk

THE WOLF TWINS
The legendary founders of ancient Rome, human twins Romulus and Remus, were supposedly suckled by a she-wolf until discovered and raised by shepherds. It is unlikely that wolf's milk could provide the nutrients required by humans.

SEARCHING FOR THE NIPPLE
A human baby, unlike many other mammals, loses weight slightly after being born, but regains birth weight by one week. In the "rooting reflex", when the baby's cheek is stroked it turns to that side, searching for the nipple – a useful, built-in behaviour for a newborn. The milk provides all the vitamins, minerals, and other nutrients, and even antibodies to protect against infectious illness.

Living in packs

HUNDREDS of mammal species, from lemmings to leopards, leave their young to make their way in the world after they have been reared by their parents. But for other mammal species, living in groups is the norm. The young may stay with their own parents for a time, as in wolves and killer whales, or the young males may move on to join other groups, as in elephants and horses. Social living has several advantages, such as hunting or defending the group as a team. In a grey wolf pack, each member knows his or her position in the scale of dominance. The only pair of wolves to mate are the dominant male and the dominant female, and after the cubs are born the father brings meat back to the den for the mother. The cubs are suckled for about ten weeks, and then the mother and the younger wolves feed them with regurgitated meat (partly digested meat returned to the mouth from the stomach) until they are old enough to start hunting with the pack. The cubs might play-fight whilst they are young, but in time, they too learn their place within the pack.

Ears are erect to show that the wolf is on the alert – either for prey or foe

EUROPEAN GREY WOLF
In earlier times there were grey wolves in every country in Europe. But these intelligent and sociable animals have been slaughtered by farmers and hunters for hundreds of years. They are now found only in limited numbers in southern and eastern Europe.

Sharp teeth enable wolf to kill its prey quickly

A WOLF OF MANY COLOURS
The Arctic wolf from the far north of Canada has a very thick, white winter coat for warmth and camouflage in the snow and ice, although it can be a shade of grey or buff, or occasionally even black during the summer. It also has a short tail and small ears to keep the body as compact as possible to reduce heat loss. Arctic wolves feed on hares and birds, and if they are lucky, a pack may be able to kill a deer or a musk ox.

LITTLE RED RIDING HOOD
When there were really wolves in the forests, parents would tell their children the story of Little Red Riding Hood to warn them against going out alone.

A RARE RED WOLF
The red wolf is smaller than the grey wolf and is adapted for living in the warmer climate of the southeastern USA. It was extinct in the wild but in 1988 a few were reintroduced into North Carolina, USA.

WINNER OR LOSER
Wolves are quick to snarl at each other when they are challenging for a position of greater seniority in the pack. But it is mostly bluff, and serious fights are rare.

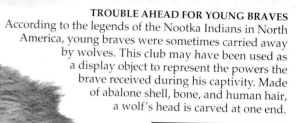

TROUBLE AHEAD FOR YOUNG BRAVES
According to the legends of the Nootka Indians in North America, young braves were sometimes carried away by wolves. This club may have been used as a display object to represent the powers the brave received during his captivity. Made of abalone shell, bone, and human hair, a wolf's head is carved at one end.

TERROR OF WEREWOLVES
According to folklore, a werewolf is a person who has changed into a wolf, or is capable of taking the shape of a wolf, while keeping its human intelligence. Many horror films have been made about werewolves.

The legs have to be long and very powerful so the wolf can range over huge distances in search of prey

A pack of wolves chase musk oxen on Ellesmere Island in the Arctic

The tail of this wolf is pointing down, showing it is rather wary of what is ahead

Living in prides

UNLIKE DOGS AND WOLVES, most types of cat, both big and small, are solitary hunters, except, that is, for the lions. The second largest of the big cats, lions live in family groups, or prides, of up to 12 animals. Because of their family support, they are the only cats which are able to kill animals larger than themselves. The role of the male lions is to defend their pride's territory. They do this by pacing around it, by roaring, and by marking trees and posts with their urine. The lionesses do most of the hunting. Each lioness gives birth every two years to about two or three cubs. If a new lioness joins a pride, the lion will usually kill any cubs she may already have before he mates with her. Similarly, when the pride's leading male becomes old and weak, he is challenged by a younger, stronger male, who then takes over and may also kill any existing cubs. This ensures the pride rears only his own offspring, not the cubs of other males.

THE KING
The lion's body posture, facial expression, and tail communicate his mood to pride members and enemies. A threatening lion will pull back his lips, and a twitching tail indicates arousal, interest, or anger.

African lion and lioness

THE PRIDE
The composition of a pride varies, but females always outnumber males. When young males reach adulthood, they either oust any older lions from the pride or, if unsuccessful, leave the pride and attach themselves to any other group of females in need of males. A pride of lions shares its territory with many other meat eaters, competing for every scrap of meat left over when the pride has had its fill.

The lioness has no mane as it would impede her efficiency as a hunter

MATE TO KING
The lionesses are the core of any pride, sticking together with close family – sisters, daughters, and aunts. The lioness has a powerful, lithe body so she can creep stealthily up to prey, before moving in for the kill.

LEO
People born under the astrological sign of Leo are said to be proud, brave, strong, and self-centred – just like the king of beasts himself.

The story of Daniel in the lions' den appears in the Old Testament

A magnificent mane, heavy body, and huge canine teeth ensure that the lion rules his world

The mane makes the lion look even bigger than he really is. It may help to frighten off other lions

THE LION AND THE UNICORN
In the Renaissance (the 15th and 16th centuries) the lion often appeared in paintings and architecture. In this beautiful French tapestry, the lion is shown to be at peace with the unicorn, symbol of purity.

HERACLES AND THE NEMEAN LION
Heracles had to perform 12 labours to pay for the killing of his family. The first was to kill the lion whose skin could not be pierced by weapons, so Heracles choked it to death. After this, he wore the skin to protect himself.

The tuft of hair at the knees makes the lion look even stronger

The still visible spots are a leftover from when the lioness was a cub

The tuft at the end of the tail is an important signal in communication when the male is challenged by a rival

Living in herds

HORSES WERE PROBABLY first domesticated for draught work and riding, over 6,000 years ago, in the Ukraine region of Europe. Gradually, wild horses were replaced by tamed ones. Today there are no truly wild horses. But there are many horses and ponies described as "feral". These feral animals are descended from domesticated stock, but are no longer under human control, and they live and breed on their own. Their behaviour and social life partly revert to the truly natural lifestyle of their distant wild ancestors. Horses are social creatures, and live in groups called herds. A herd has the harem type of social organization, with a chief stallion who gathers and protects several mares and their young. Today, some feral horses, such as the American mustang and Australian brumby, are controlled by hunting, or rounded up and domesticated.

FELL PONIES
In Britain there are many breeds of pony that live on the moors, such as the Fell pony. Although Fell ponies are owned, they are allowed to live and breed with very little human control. Traditionally, the Fell ponies have been used as pack ponies, for riding, and for light draught work.

Well-proportioned head

Long face and large nose give an exceptionally keen sense of smell for detecting predators

GERMAN DÜLMEN
These rare ponies live semi-wild on the Duke of Croy's estate in Westphalia in Germany. They have been bred with both British and Polish ponies, so they are not pure-bred. The herd dates back to the early 1300s.

THE BRUMBY OF AUSTRALIA
For 150 years there have been herds of feral horses in Australia, ever since they were abandoned during the gold rush. These horses, called brumbies, formed herds and reproduced in great numbers over large areas. They are unpopular with cattle and sheep ranchers because they compete for grazing, and usually carry many parasites. Since the 1960s, they have been hunted so extensively that there are now very few. A brumby stallion will defend his herd by kicking and biting with great vigour.

Long legs for running fast on the open grasslands, where horses first evolved

Well-formed foot with strong horn on hoof

SYMBOLIC HORSES
A wild running horse has often been used as a symbol of speed, power, freedom, and elegance. It has advertised many things, from banks to sports cars – such as the Mustang and Pinto in the USA, and (as shown here) the Ferrari, the supreme speedster.

THE MUSTANGS OF AMERICA
The feral horses, or mustangs, of the Nevada desert in the USA have hard lives travelling great distances in search of enough grass and water to live on.

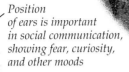

DAWN IN THE CAMARGUE
The beautiful white horses from the Camargue in the south of France have lived wild in the marshes of the Rhône delta for over 1,000 years. They have very wide hooves for living on soft wet grassland.

Star

Position of ears is important in social communication, showing fear, curiosity, and other moods

Long, straight, full mane

Like its ears, a horse's tail is an important social signal, as well as a useful fly whisk

Snip

Egg-shaped eye can simultaneously focus on grass and on distant horizon to watch for enemies

Blaze

Deep chest with large heart and lungs give great stamina for sustained fast running

THE PONIES OF THE NEW FOREST
There have been herds of ponies living in the New Forest of Hampshire, England, since the 11th century. For 800 years these ponies lived wild, until attempts were made in the 19th century to improve them by bringing in stallions of other breeds. They still run semi-wild in their native area, but are also reared on stud farms to provide ideal riding and working ponies.

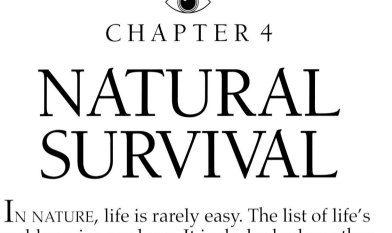

CHAPTER 4
NATURAL SURVIVAL

IN NATURE, life is rarely easy. The list of life's problems is very long. It includes bad weather, harsh seasons, famine, drought, predators, competitors, pests, and parasites. Animals overcome these problems by a countless variety of means.

AUSTRALIAN HORN SHARK
Port Jackson sharks live on the sea bed in shallow water. Many often gather in the same area where they rest on the sandy floors of caves or channels between rocks. These may offer protection against currents.

AS BRIGHT AS THE BACKGROUND
Many coral reef fish, such as these adult (with yellow tail) and young emperor angelfish, have intensely bright colours and patterns. Isolated, as here, they seem to be inviting predation. But their natural habitat is among the equally colourful corals, seaweeds, crabs, and sponges of the reef. And while they stay together in a shoal, it is difficult for a predator to pick one out clearly to attack it.

AS DULL AS THE BACKGROUND
In great contrast to the coral reef, the shallow sea bed in other places is dull shades of green or brown, with sand, mud, and pebbles. The spotted ray is at home here, camouflaged to blend in perfectly, thereby aiding survival.

MAKING FRIENDS
Some different species help each other.
These clownfish are protected
by the sea anemones' stinging
tentacles in return for
leftover scraps of food.

Resisting attack

SOME ANIMALS ARE UNLIKELY to become prey. No creature is likely to attack a tiger, eagle, crocodile, or shark. These beasts are large and powerful and well equipped with teeth, claws, and other weapons. They are called top carnivores, which means that in terms of food chains and food webs, they are at the summit – they can eat what they like, but nothing eats them. For the majority of animals, especially the smaller ones, a vital part of the survival game is to avoid becoming prey. There are several basic strategies: to remain quite still in the hope of not being noticed, an option which is greatly helped by being camouflaged; to escape, by fleeing at high speed; to hide in a crack or crevice; or to fight back fiercely. The first strategy has two important advantages. It uses very little energy, and it is less likely to end in physical conflict.

ATTACK AND...
A crab will usually hide under a boulder or among seaweeds. If approached out in the open, it has a well-rehearsed set of actions, as shown by this common crab. It holds its pincers forward threateningly, then rears up as though about to attack. This crab has already had a close encounter, since it has lost a leg.

STAY THEN FLEE
The day gecko, a lizard from Madagascar, lives among the bright green leaves of rainforest trees. It is difficult to spot there, because of its excellent camouflage. The gecko may even sway with the leaves to improve its disguise. As soon as it thinks it has been noticed, the gecko races away with astonishing speed and agility.

The gecko cleans its face and eyes with its tongue

Gaps between the scales allow the gecko to bend its body

Poisonous sting

NO NEED TO FLEE
Most animals know not to mess with a scorpion. This eight-legged creature is an arachnid, a relative of the spiders. When approached, the scorpion turns to face the enemy. It holds out its strong pincers threateningly and arches its tail over its head. This brings the sharp venomous sting into full view. Most scorpions use the sting mainly in self-defence. Some may use its poison to subdue struggling prey.

Missing leg

Pincers raised in mock attack

Crouched and curled up in defence

Preparing to escape

...THEN RETREAT
Most enemies think
again when confronted
by spirited resistance.
When the enemy
hesitates, the crab
lowers itself, ready to
curl into a protective
ball, and then begins
to crawl off sideways.

*A claw on each toe
gives extra grip*

*The underside of the
toes are covered
with tiny bristles
for grip*

A fighting chance

A CREATURE MAY HAVE FINE physical defences, such as hard armour or sharp spines. It may have powerful chemical defences, such as an appalling smell or foul-tasting flesh. But none of these is much use in the struggle for survival, unless the animal has the right behaviour to go with it. Evolution shapes a living thing's size, colour, and other physical features. It also shapes an animal's actions and behaviour patterns. The most important behaviours are instinctive, or in-built. The creature can perform the actions without having to learn what to do and how to do it by trial and error.

Red threads shoot out from the tails to scare off enemies

Sharp barbs on the tails are a further deterrent to enemies

The caterpillar breathes through tiny holes in the side of its body called spiracles

The pattern on the caterpillar's body camouflages it against the branches and leaves among which it lives

1 TAKE-OFF
This North American leopard frog is showing how to make a long graceful leap away from an enemy. The powerful back legs provide the physical means to jump to safety, but the frog must be able to move them and the rest of its body in a smooth and co-ordinated fashion. At take-off, it presses its feet against the ground, closes its eyes for protection, and holds its front legs near the body for extra streamlining.

DEADLY BEAUTY
The lionfish has no need to swim fast and escape. It swims along lazily, even when approached by another animal. Its fins are armed with deadly poison. Predators recognize the bright colours as a warning signal, and stay away.

2 IN MID FLIGHT
The frog stretches its rear legs to their full length. The eyes and mouth are still closed.

Bright red patch exposed when the caterpillar is threatened

3 LANDING
The frog breaks the water's surface with a big splash and a loud plop, which distracts its enemies. It opens its eyes at once to check what is under the water, and reaches upwards to take a quick gulp of air at the surface. It holds its front legs out to act as brakes. The back legs are about to bend up towards the body, ready for another powerful push – this time against the water – for a speedy swimming stroke away from danger. During the whole leap, every detailed movement of the frog's body is finely tuned for maximum effect.

Head drawn back into the thorax

Short antennae can tell which leaves are good to eat

True legs with special hooks for gripping food

INSTINCT FOR SURVIVAL
Insects are small and relatively simple animals with short lives. They have little time or ability to learn, so they have a whole battery of instinctive behaviours to help their survival. This puss moth caterpillar suddenly draws its head back into its body, revealing a vivid red circle with two black spots. These look startlingly like the eyes of a larger creature. At the same time the caterpillar flicks its two "tails" forwards, and a fine red thread whips out from each. Then the caterpillar rears up and squirts out stinging formic acid from a gland under its head. Few predators can get past this multi-defence.

Sensing the surroundings

NO ROAD SENSE
Like most wild animals, frogs and toads do not understand the danger of road traffic. However, drivers can help by taking care. Road signs like this warn motorists about migrating frogs and toads.

O NE OF THE CHARACTERISTIC FEATURES of any animal is its ability to detect what is happening in its surroundings, and to react appropriately to ensure survival. Many animals have the same five main senses as we do – sight, hearing, touch, taste, and smell. Amphibians show these senses very well, since they are adapted for life on land, and in the water. Some creatures, amphibians included, have extra senses, such as the ability to detect the Earth's magnetic field, or to pick up the tiny electrical signals made by the contracting muscles of an active animal.

Tentacle

MYSTERY SENSE ORGAN
The worm-like amphibians called caecilians have a small tentacle below the eye. Its function is unknown, but it may be for picking up vibrations by touch, or for detecting food, predators, or a mate by smell.

FEELING THE PRESSURE
Frogs and toads that spend a lot of time in water have a lateral line – a sense system for detecting pressure changes in the water made by moving or stationary objects. The individual sense organs of the lateral line, called plaques, are easily seen on the head and along the sides of the body on this African clawed toad.

Lateral line

Lateral line

Eye of mandarin salamander (below)

Eye of marbled newt (below)

SIGHT
It is a safe guess that the larger an animal's eyes, the more it relies on eyesight. The mandarin salamander relies on vision to spot slow-moving prey in poor light. The marbled newt hunts more in water and so uses sight, smell, and taste.

TADPOLES TOO
Lateral line systems are also found in aquatic newts, salamanders, sirens, and amphibian larvae, like this American bullfrog tadpole. Its position and development varies in different species.

TOUCH

Sensitivity to touch is usually greatest on an animal's extremities, such as its hands, feet, nose, lips, and ears. The Surinam toad has long, thin tubular fingers, and the skin on them is packed with touch-sensitive nerve endings, rather like our own. The toad feels with these for worms, insect larvae, fish, and other prey in the muddy beds of rivers and streams. The fingers are covered with tiny spines that help to grip the prey.

(1) Vertical pupil of red-eyed tree frog

TEMPERATURE CONTROL

Moist-skinned animals such as amphibians and worms rapidly lose body water by evaporation in hot or dry conditions. They sense temperature levels and sudden dryness through their skin and control their body temperature by basking in the sun if too cold, or moving into the shade if too hot. This painted reed frog of South Africa is reducing the area of its body exposed to the sun, by tucking in its legs.

(2) Heart-shaped pupil of Oriental fire-bellied toad

PERFECT PUPILS

Eye colour and pupil shape are very variable in amphibians and other animals: (1) vertical, cat-like for night vision or quick response to rapidly changing light conditions; (2) heart-shaped; (3) horizontal (the more common pupil for normal daylight vision); and (4) round.

(3) Horizontal pupil of Asian tree toad

(4) Round pupil of Madagascan tomato frog

Ear of American bullfrog

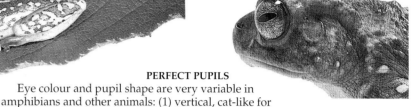

HEARING

The basic design for an animal ear is a thin, taut membrane which vibrates when sound waves hit it – the eardrum. A frog's ears are plainly visible behind its eyes.

SMELL

Airborne chemicals are detected by a furry, hair-like olfactory organ inside the nose. Smells give information about food, enemies, and mates – the male newt wafts a mating scent from a gland at the base of its tail towards a female.

Camouflage

Black form

Speckled form

Peppered moth resting on a tree

THE THEME OF CAMOUFLAGE crops up again and again in this book because it does in nature. Colours and patterns that enable an animal to blend in with its surroundings are called cryptic (hiding) coloration. Creatures may mimic another object which is inedible, such as a twig, or distasteful, such as droppings. Or they may take on patterns and colours of local trees, rocks, or leaves. Because they are especially vulnerable in daylight hours, small edible animals, such as caterpillars and resting moths, have perfected the art of concealment. Butterflies, which are active by day, and which usually rest with their wings together over their backs, have adopted other forms of camouflage. Some forest butterflies rest like moths with their wings spread out, while other species disguise themselves as either living or decaying leaves.

CITY MOTH, COUNTRY MOTH
Some years ago, it was realized that the city form of the European peppered moth had gradually changed from a light to a black colour. This helped them escape birds, which could easily spot a light-coloured moth on a smoke-polluted tree. In the countryside the same moth is still speckled white.

Wing looks like a torn leaf

DAMAGED LEAF
To make its camouflage more realistic, this Pyralid moth from South America has irregularly shaped clear areas in its wings. When the moth is resting these give the impression of a damaged leaf.

DECAYING LEAF
This South American leaf moth has a dead leaf pattern on its wings, including a "skeletonized" part. When resting, the moth rolls the front part of its wings to resemble a leaf stalk.

Resemblance to stalk and veins of a leaf

INDIAN LEAF TRICK
The most dramatic example of butterfly camouflage is this Indian leaf butterfly. It frequently rests on the ground in leaf litter, where it becomes virtually invisible.

Brown underside of leaf butterfly

Orange and blue upper side of leaf butterfly

DEAD OR ALIVE?

One of these dead leaves is the Indian leaf butterfly in its cryptic pose. Would you have noticed it in the speckly shade of a woodland? The butterfly must remain perfectly still, or the effect is spoiled – showing how behaviour is also important for good camouflage.

Wings look like wood

Wings look like a dead leaf

When at rest, the underside of the butterfly's wings are exposed, making it look like a decaying leaf

VANISHING MOTHS

These two moths from South America are in their normal resting position and show how successful their camouflage is. In order to survive, they must not look like moths or they would soon be detected by a hungry bird or lizard.

DEADLY ENEMIES

One of the main reasons why many moths and butterflies are camouflaged is to escape from predatory birds. Since birds hunt mainly by sight, rather than by sound or scent, the cryptic colours have to be especially accurate to fool them.

Light crusty-looking patches mimic the lichens which grow on old tree bark

WOOD BORER

The caterpillar of this carpenter moth from Central America bores into trees. As an adult, the moth would be almost invisible against this bark.

Patterns of life

ANIMALS ARE NOT ONLY CAMOUFLAGED to blend in with their surroundings. Some have specially shaped appendages which add to the effect, such as the twig-shaped legs of the stick insect. Some animals can also change their own body pattern and coloration to merge in with the surroundings in which they happen to be. Among these quick-change artists are certain beetles and other insects, cuttlefish and squid, flatfish such as the plaice and sole, and reptiles such as the chameleon.

COLOUR CONSCIOUS
Lizards, especially chameleons, are truly masters of camouflage. Many can make the colour of their skin lighter or darker as needed. Although these changes take place so that the chameleon can match its background, many other things influence the colour change. Light level, temperature, and the mood of the lizard (for example if it is frightened) can all affect the colour it takes on. The chameleon's skin has several layers of colour cells. Beneath these are the melanophores, cells with tentacle-like arms which extend through the other layers.

The colour change is caused by the melanophores moving a dark brown pigment in and out of the upper layers of the skin

LEAF GREEN
Hard to spot against the palm trees on which they are commonly found, these tree skinks live in the forests of Indonesia, the Philippines, and the Solomon Islands. Their bright green and mottled brown bodies make them almost invisible. Green is a popular colour among tree-living animals active in the day.

FLOWER POWER
The head may be small, but beneath the leaves is the large body of a Murray River turtle from eastern Australia. The waterweed helps to hide the body of this powerful carnivore.

DOUBLE TROUBLE

Lying still in the leaf litter of the forests of tropical Africa, these gaboon vipers are nearly invisible in the dappled light and shade, as they wait for rodents, frogs, and birds. The snake shape is disguised by the disruptive coloration and pattern. Yet when one of the snakes is removed from its natural background, its vivid markings become strikingly obvious. Although unaggressive and unlikely to attack, this viper's bite would be dangerously venomous to anyone unfortunate enough to tread on one! In fact, the fangs of the gaboon viper are the longest of any snake – up to 50 mm (2 in) in a 1.80 m (6 ft) specimen.

Gaboon viper

HIDDEN DEPTHS

Luckily for this black caiman, it could be mistaken for rocks as it lies in the muddy waters. It is hunted for its skin and is constantly threatened. But its ability to lie unseen helps it when it is looking for food.

127

Hiding in the open

SMALL PLANT-EATING MAMMALS are vulnerable when feeding out in the open. They cannot take food back to a nest or burrow easily and their diet is usually not very nutritious, so they must spend long periods eating. Camouflage is therefore very important. A body covering of small parts or units with variable colours produces the best effect. The hairs on some insect and spider bodies, the tiny scales on butterfly wings, the scales on fish and reptiles, the feathers of birds, and the fur of mammals are all well suited to this purpose. A pattern may help to break up the body outline of some animals. This is called disruptive coloration.

BUILT-IN CAMOUFLAGE
The two-toed sloth of South America is very slow-moving and often completely still. In the dim forest light it merges with the foliage because it has green algae growing on its coat. Its long outer guard hairs have grooves on them in which the algae grow.

PEBBLE WITH WHISKERS
Small rodents such as mice and voles are among the most vulnerable of all animals. Their main defences are sharp senses and a quick dive into a nearby burrow, or good camouflage if stranded out in the open. This Arabian spiny mouse's fur blends with the dry sand, light-coloured pebbles, and parched wood of its semi-desert home.

Extra-thick spiky hairs on its back give the spiny mouse its name

128

LEAF WITH A TAIL

Meadow voles live in a variety of places, from grassland to woods and streambanks. They forage on the ground, which is usually littered with dead or dying leaves and other plant parts. Voles are very busy animals, being active more or less round the clock, so visual camouflage is very important. A vole alerted by the soft wing-beat of a hunting bird might "freeze" in its tracks. In the dim light of dawn or dusk, or in the dappled shade under the trees, it would be difficult to spot from above – as shown by this owl's-eye view.

Leaves are from a deciduous woodland

Dead leaves and bits of wood form a dark background against which the vole is hidden

HIDING FROM THE ENEMY

Humans at war imitate nature and camouflage themselves, their vehicles, and weapons. Standard combat clothes are natural greens and browns, mottled and patched to break up the soldier's outline in woods and scrubland. Snow-country outfits must be white, like the coats of Arctic foxes, hares, and ptarmigans.

DISGUISING THE OUTLINE

The Malayan tapir's striking coloration of white back and belly, and black everything else, is a fine example of disruptive coloration. In the dark night-time forest the pattern breaks up the tapir's bulky body outline, making its distinctive shape less recognizable to predators. The young tapir is dappled white, a similarly disruptive device.

129

Not what they seem

SOME OF THE MOST COLOURFUL creatures are advertising their defences to aid their survival. They have a poisonous bite or sting, or a foul smell, or they taste horrible. This is called warning coloration. Some animals with warning colours have no proper defences at all. They are mimics copying the patterns of the truly dangerous animals so that predators avoid them too. This type of mimicry is called Batesian mimicry after the naturalist Henry Bates. It occurs especially among tropical butterflies and other insects. Mimics must not become common, because the effect of the colours on predators will weaken.

BUTTERFLY BATES
Henry Walter Bates (1825-1892) was one of the first European explorer-naturalists to study in distant parts of the world. He worked in the forests of South America, collecting butterflies, beetles, and other creatures, and sending them back to museums for description and cataloguing. His work on mimicry was an important factor in Charles Darwin's ideas about evolution.

Mimic
Dismorphia butterfly

Distasteful
Methona butterfly

Small
postman butterfly

— *Flesh tastes unpleasant because the butterfly, especially as a caterpillar, feeds on poisonous plants*

Postman
butterfly

Mimic
Gazera moth

PRETEND POSTMAN
The small postman butterfly from western Brazil has red-on-black – a common combination of warning colours – coupled with light forewing patches. These inform about its poisonous flesh. A close cousin, the postman butterfly, flies in the same rainforest. It has the same warning coloration, but it is not unpalatable; it is quite edible. The postman is an impersonator. It mimics the small postman to gain protection against predation.

MORE THAN ONE MIMIC
The *Methona* butterfly in the middle of these three insects has a distasteful body, and shows off the fact with its distinctive wing patterns. The *Dismorphia* butterfly at the top looks amazingly similar, but it is a mimic, and not distasteful at all. Neither is the *Gazera* insect at the bottom; it is not even a butterfly. It is an edible moth pretending to be an inedible butterfly.

WASPISH LOOK-ALIKE
This hoverfly is striped
black and yellow to look like
a wasp, but it has no sting. It
lives and feeds among flowers
and rotting fruit just like real wasps,
so most predators leave it alone.

*Black and yellow
stripes are common
warning colours in the
animal world*

*Hoverflies use their
wings to hover in the
air, then dart off
quickly, and they can
move in any direction,
including backwards*

AVOIDING PREDATION
The caterpillar of the china-mark
moth, from Europe and Asia, gets
over the problem of predation by
adopting a very unusual home. It
builds a shelter on the underside
of a leaf of a water plant, and
hides in there while it eats.

Dry
season form

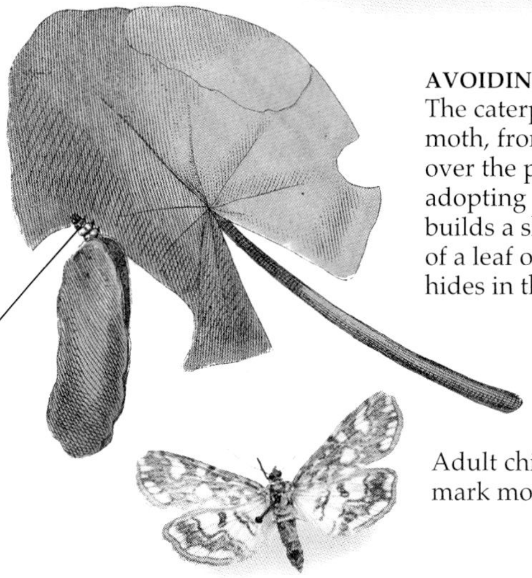

*Caterpillar
in shelter*

*Adult china-
mark moth*

*Wings are clear
because they have
fewer scales than
other butterflies
and moths*

Wet
season form

*Spots on hind wings
resemble the eyes of
a predator such as
a cat, hawk, or owl*

SEASONAL SWITCH
Although these two butterflies look very
different, they are in fact both pansy butterflies
from Africa. The pansy has a different pattern if
it develops in the wet rather than the dry season.
This switch of colours may help to prevent
predators getting to know the butterflies,
and so make them continually cautious.

GHOST OF THE RAINFOREST
This clearwing butterfly flits through the forests of South
and Central America. It has not evolved bright colours to
forewarn of poisonous or distasteful flesh. Instead, it has
gone for the "disappearing act". This butterfly is almost
invisible both in flight and at rest, due to its ghostly, almost
transparent, wings. Even so, its wings do have eyespots, to
mimic the appearance of a larger predator.

DISAPPEARING ACT
The Spanish spadefoot toad gets its name from the black, horny "spades" on its feet, which it uses to dig into sand or soft earth. It can shuffle its feet alternately to dig vertical burrows.

Spade foot

1 UNDERCOVER AGENT
This Asian bullfrog is fairly typical in its habit of moving backwards into cover. Hiding reduces the likelihood of being eaten or drying out. For this animal it is also a means of increasing the camouflage effect while lying in wait for passing food.

2 MOVING BACK
The colour pattern on the frog's back is similar to that of the mosses and leaf litter of its surroundings. A shuffling movement of the back feet takes it backwards, down into the litter.

ODD FROG OUT
This burrowing frog from Mexico is a "feet-first" burrower, like the spadefoot toad (above), and many mammal diggers, such as the wombat and armadillo.

Getting out of sight

IF AN ANIMAL IS NOT SPEEDY enough to escape from predators, or its camouflage is ineffective, there is another possible survival strategy – to hide out of sight. In dense undergrowth this may be fairly easy, but out in the open, the only option is to dig down into the ground. Creatures as diverse as beetles, millipedes, desert skinks, snakes, wombats, shellfish, frogs, and toads can burrow their way to concealment and safety. Even some fishes burrow, flapping with their fins and tail to burrow into the mud or sand on the sea bed. Some animals burrow to avoid the heat of the sun, intense cold, or drying winds. This type of dugout is only temporary, and the animal will surface again when the danger is passed. Another array of animals, from moles to earthworms, live underground for most of their lives.

3 GOING . . .
The frog continues to bed itself into the litter, helping to cover its shape. It may pause at times to feel how comfortable it is.

4 GOING . . .
The back legs have disappeared. Now it is the turn of the front legs to be pushed back and forth in the leaf litter, moving small pieces of leaf over the body.

Most of the frog is still visible

132

The South African spotted shovel-nosed frog

HEAD FIRST

The spotted shovel-nosed frog from South Africa is a "head first" burrower with a difference – it actually uses its head, or rather its snout, for burrowing. The body is bent forward, head down, with the back legs held straight, pushing the frog's snout forwards into the soil. Digging is done by raising and lowering the snout, and by scraping soil away with the powerful hands.

6 GONE
Only the head is showing. The frog has gained several advantages by its activity. It is well concealed and comfortable and its moist skin is protected from the drying effect of wind. Also, by staying still, the frog will not lose weight by burning energy chasing after food. All it has to do now is wait for its prey to walk by.

5 ABOUT TO GO
The legs and back half of the body are now hidden. The wriggling movements continue; the body is rotated, pushing it down into the leaf litter.

Only the frog's head is visible

A spiny coat

A SPIKY SYSTEM OF SELF-DEFENCE is employed by a huge range of animals from the hedgehog shown here, to the porcupine fish, lizards such as the thorny devil, sea urchins and starfish, and insects such as thornbugs and prickly mantises. Many plants are also spiny for exactly the same reason – to ward off predators. Each of the 5,000 or so spines covering the Eurasian hedgehog is a hair modified during evolution into a sharp, stiff spike about 2-3 cm (1 in) long. As with any form of self-defence, the hedgehog's behaviour has evolved in tandem with its spines, so that when in trouble it rolls into a ball shape and waits for danger to pass.

As danger passes, the head and front legs emerge

3 ALL CLEAR
The hedgehog has decided that the main threat is over and now is the time to leave. Its head straightens and is first to protrude from the ball, so that the animal can smell, hear, and see clearly. Also beginning to emerge are its front legs. The hedgehog has surprisingly long legs, usually obscured under its mantle of spines. It can run well, burrow, clamber over low walls, and swim when it needs to.

Hedgehog cautiously begins to unroll

2 CAUTIOUS PEEP
The spines physically intimidate the enemy, and they also act as a springy cushion should the hedgehog be pushed down a slope or against a tree. After a few moments of calm, the hedgehog relaxes slightly and peeks out of its prickly protection. Its eyesight is relatively poor, but its sense of smell is keen. Also, vibrations in the ground made by a creature moving nearby are transmitted via the spines and felt in the skin.

Fully rolled hedgehog has no vulnerable parts

1 ALL-OVER PROTECTION
In the face of danger, the hedgehog quickly tucks in its head, legs, and tail, and arches its back into a U-shape. A "cloak" of muscle under the loose skin comes down over the head, sides, and rear. A band of muscle running around the edge of this cloak contracts, acting like a drawstring to pull the mantle of spines together around the underparts. The spines are automatically erected in the process. This defensive behaviour produces the tight ball that presents nothing but spines to the molester.

DEADLY ENEMY
The fox hunts many smaller mammals, including hedgehogs. It may poke and prod at a tightly rolled hedgehog for some time, in an attempt to make the animal uncurl and run off, whereupon the fox claws at the vulnerable belly.

STRANGE BEHAVIOUR
Hedgehogs have often been seen to chew something foul, such as a dead toad, and then flick and spit their frothy saliva over their spines. It is not clear why. One theory is that this "self-anointing" is part of the animal's defence, helping to deter predators.

Head remains tucked under

Feet barely visible

BABY'S DEFENCE
A baby hedgehog's first coat of rubbery spines lies flat under its skin at birth, but pops up within a few hours. The baby cannot roll up until it is 11 days old. Its main defence is to jerk its head upwards, stabbing predators on the nose.

4 FLIP-OVER
Should the hedgehog continue to unroll while lying on its back, its vulnerable underparts would be exposed to any predators. To prevent attack, the hedgehog executes a quick flip-over manoeuvre to land on its belly, keeping its feet tucked in and its head well down for continued protection.

5 PREPARING TO MOVE OFF
If there is no sign of renewed threat, the hedgehog uncurls further. Its head emerges to reveal which end is which. Sniffing, and with whiskers quivering, it looks about for a suitable refuge, preferably a dark tangle of brambles and undergrowth.

Head emerges to investigate surroundings

6 QUICK EXIT
Defence gives way to escape, and the hedgehog scurries off to safety. With its body held off the ground, the animal can move surprisingly fast when at risk – at about the speed of a human's quick walk. But when foraging peacefully for slugs, worms, insects, and fallen fruit, it stays lower on the ground and shuffles among the leaves and vegetation.

HEDGEHOG RELATIVE
The echidna of Australia and New Guinea has a coat of defensive spines similar to those of the hedgehog. Yet it is only distantly related, having evolved the same system of defence separately. The hedgehog gives birth to live young, like nearly all other mammals. The echidna is one of two mammals that lay eggs (the other being the platypus) and the babies hatch from these.

Surprising the enemy

THE PORCUPINE FISH, like the hedgehog on the previous page, uses its prickles for self-defence. But it has an added element, which is very important in many survival strategies – that of surprise. When untroubled, this fish's spines lay almost flat and inconspicuous against its body. As soon as the fish senses threat or danger, it swallows water and, within a second or two, swells up like a balloon, erecting its spines and showing more of its bright colours in the process. To a hopeful predator, a potential meal becomes a huge, glaring, prickly ball, too big and spiky to tackle. The predator pauses and the moment is lost. The element of surprise aids survival in many situations.

THE SURGEON'S SCALPEL
Surgeonfish are colourful inhabitants of coral reefs throughout the tropical Pacific. The name comes from a sharp, bony, blade-like "lancet" on either side of the body, near the base of the tail. These blades cut flesh as cleanly as a surgeon's scalpel. In some species there is a row of small blades; in others the lancets lie folded in a groove when not in use, but can be flicked out for use, like flick knives. Surgeonfish use their razors mainly for defence, lashing out at predators in a surprise counter-attack. Most of the time they graze among the coral and weeds, rowing along with their pectoral fins.

Surgeonfish

Dorsal fin

Pectoral fins

Tall, thin, deep-bodied shape

Long anal fin

Lancet blade

Lancet blade extended at right angles to the fish

Spines lie flat along the body when the fish is at rest

GOING UP
There are several species of porcupine fish, which live mainly in tropical seas. They are about 60-90 cm (24-35 in) long and favour shallow water, especially beds of sea grass, where they catch and crunch up their prey of small crabs, sea urchins, starfish, and shellfish. Close relatives are the pufferfish, which have a similar ability to blow themselves up. A deflated or "relaxed" porcupine fish looks much like many other fish, although it has rather prominent eyes. If a porcupine fish is taken from the water suddenly, it can take in air instead of water to inflate itself. When the danger has passed, the fish slowly lets itself down again.

Spines swivel out to stand at right angles to body when porcupine fish is inflated

Normal (deflated) shape of pufferfish

Pufferfish inflated to full extent to intimidate enemy

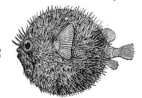

Pale underside colour is more pronounced when the fish is inflated

OUT OF PUFF
These before-and-after views of a pufferfish show how the length of the fish remains unchanged after puffing up.

Displays for defence

HAVE YOU EVER accidentally disturbed a wild animal, and jumped as it hissed or postured at you, before it made off? Defence displays involve exaggerated body positions, showing off colours, spines, frills, and flaps. Other tactics designed to intimidate and scare the enemy are hissing, growling, spitting, nasty smells, and mock attacks, all done at speed for the added advantage of surprise. The aim is to frighten the foe and then make a getaway, because when the real fighting starts, survival for one or even both opponents rapidly becomes less likely. Certain features, such as the sound of a hiss, or the colours of red and yellow, seem to work right through the animal world. They are used and understood by creatures as varied as insects, scorpions, reptiles, birds, and mammals.

ON GUARD

One of the most spectacular defence displays is that of the Australian frilled lizard. This reptile is about 1 m (3 ft) long including its tail, and lives in the dry scrub where it eats grasshoppers and other small prey. The "frill" is a large flap of loose skin which is attached to the neck and is normally kept folded flat. When startled by a predator, the lizard erects this ruff-like collar, so that it is often more than four times the width of its body. If challenged, the lizard will also start to bob its head, lash its tail, hiss loudly, and wave its legs about.

Gaping mouth expands the neck frill – the wider the mouth is opened, the more erect the frill becomes

STINKY STINKPOT

The skunk is a mammal that is well known for the foul smell it produces when frightened or threatened. The stinkpot from the USA is a turtle that is just as evil-smelling as its name suggests. The smell is produced by a pair of glands in the soft skin of the turtle's thighs. Apart from being very smelly when frightened, it is also aggressive, so it is unlikely to be set upon by too many predators.

Tail is lashed back and forth

Frill fully erected to scare aggressors

Stinkpot

Skunk

Extended claws and flexed feet provide strong balance

ADD-ON SURVIVAL

The survival features and behaviour of most animals are adapted to their natural habitat. They would not succeed in unfamiliar environments. Humans can survive almost anywhere, due to our inventions of protective clothing and other aids.

THE TALE OF A TAIL

When grabbed by the tail, some animals – especially lizards and birds – will shed it. Although a dramatic method of defence, loss of a tail is better than certain death. Several lizards waggle their tail when first attacked and this helps to confuse the attacking animal. The vertebrae, or small back bones, along the tail have special cracks marking the spots where it can break off. When the tail is grasped, the muscles, which are also arranged so that they will separate neatly, contract. This causes one of the vertebrae to break off.

Fracture points along the tail

1 BREAKING FREE

This tree skink has lost part of its tail while breaking free from a predator. The shed part of the tail often twitches for several minutes after it has been severed, interesting the enemy for long enough for the lizard to escape.

Tail has been recently shed

Although the new tail looks the same on the outside, it has a simple tube of cartilage instead of vertebrae on the inside

2 GROWING STRONGER

In two months the tail has noticeably grown back. Losing it was quite costly, however. The lizard may have been storing food in it for a time when there might be little or none around, such as in winter or during a dry season. Some species are also known to live longer when they have a complete tail.

3 NEW FOR OLD

After eight months the tail has almost grown to its original full length. If necessary, the tail can be broken off again, but it will only be able to break in the old part, where there are still vertebrae and "cracking points".

Growing a new tail uses up a lot of energy that could have been put to better use

PLAYING DEAD

When all else fails, animals such as possums and some snakes pretend to be dead. When this European grass snake first meets an enemy it puffs and hisses loudly. If this does not work, the snake rolls over on its back, wriggles (as though in the last stages of death) and then lies quite still, with its mouth wide open and its tongue hanging out. Although pretending to be dead may fool some animals, the snake repeats the trick if turned over, rather giving the game away!

Warning colours

A FEATURE THAT SOME ANIMALS HAVE to help them survive is poisonous (toxic) or horrible-tasting flesh. Many animals have poison for self-defence rather than for catching prey, although some animals have both. Would-be predators are made aware of this by the vivid patterns, known as warning colours, which poisonous animals wear. Some of the brightest belong to the poison-dart frogs and mantella frogs of tropical forests.

DANDY FROG
This exquisitely dressed frog, looking just like a poison-dart frog in his clothes of many colours, is all puffed up and in his Sunday best.

Bright colour helps to warn off predators

Red flash colour helps camouflage frog

This bright mantella has a red "flash" colour on the inside of its leg

This yellow mantella shows up clearly in the forest and is easily recognized as poisonous

STRANGE NAME
This species was given its common name – strawberry poison-dart frog – because of its strawberry-red colour, made even brighter by deep blue-black flecks. But strawberry poison-dart frogs from different areas may be blue, green, yellow, orange, plain, spotted, and even black and white.

Mantellas have many colour varieties so they are very difficult to identify

WAR PAINT
Some native peoples of North America used war paint to strike terror into the hearts of their enemies. This Hopi Indian chief wears orange, red, and yellow – the classic warning colours – in his headdress. Animals use the same colours to frighten away their enemies.

GOLDEN LOOK-ALIKE
This golden-yellow poison-dart frog has highly toxic skin. It is closely related and looks very similar to *Phyllobates terribilis* – the most toxic of all frogs.

Golden mantella from Madagascar

This green
mantella
was first
described
scientifically in 1988.
It comes from Madagascar.
New animal species are
still being discovered in
remote places.

FASCINATING FROGS

Poison-dart frogs make
up a fascinating group. Some
are brightly coloured and highly
poisonous, having complex chemicals
in their skin. They range in size from 1.5 cm
(0.6 in) long, to up to 5 cm (2 in) long, like these
two. Poison-darts are social animals, with complex
territorial, courtship, and mating behaviours.

Bright black
and red stripes
make this frog
more visible, to
warn off enemies

LIFE IN THE PENTHOUSE

This spotted poison-dart
frog was discovered in 1984.
It is found 15–20 m (48–65 ft)
up in the treetops of the
cloud forests of Panama.
There may be many
more high-level, tree-living
species of animals
waiting to be discovered.

POISONED DARTS

The Choco Indians,
who live in western
Colombia in South
America, poison the
tips of the blow-
pipe darts they use
for hunting. They
obtain the toxin by
heating a live frog
over a campfire.
Only a few species
are used, but one is
so poisonous that
the dart has only to
be wiped against
the live frog's back
for it to be deadly.

Poison-dart
frogs are social
animals, living
in small groups

HAWAIIAN HOLIDAY

This metallic-
green poison-
dart frog from
Costa Rica,
Panama, and
Colombia has
been introduced
into the islands
of Hawaii and,
like some of the
other species, has also
been bred in captivity.

*When colours
develop, the poison
develops too*

TOXIC TADPOLES

Poison-dart frogs
carry their tadpoles to
small isolated pools,
often one at a time,
where they develop
their colours and
skin poisons as
they grow.

INSECT SIZE AND SOUND

At less than 2 cm (0.75 in), this is one of
the smallest poison-dart frogs. It lives in
isolated patches of forest in the Andes
mountains and its scientific name means
"buzzer" – after its insect-like call.

Yellow and black
are common warning
colours in frogs,
snakes, salamanders,
wasps, and bees.

Underwater poison

On LAND, a self-defensive toxin that simply oozes out on the skin, as in frogs and toads, is very effective. But in water, the poison would be rapidly diluted and washed away. So aquatic creatures often have self-defence systems where the poison is jabbed or injected into the enemy by a spike or a spine. Or they may even have poison incorporated into their flesh. Fish show both of these methods, coupled with warning coloration to advertise their venomous chemical defence.

The stargazer's poison spines are above its pectoral fins

Thin, whippy tail is of little use for swimming, but is excellent as a stinging tool

Delicate patterned tail

Three venomous anal spines

Sting is a spine-shaped, iron-hard "dagger" of bone set into the tail

Dinner or death?

Some fish have flesh that is poisonous to eat. Certain types of pufferfish are especially toxic. But the poison, tetrodotoxin, is limited to specific body parts of the fish. The flesh itself is said to be relatively safe and quite tasty. In Japan, pufferfish is served in restaurants as the delicacy "fugu", where specially trained chefs prepare and cook the catch. Even so, despite various safeguards, death has occurred when fugu has been prepared incorrectly.

Dead pufferfish awaiting preparation

A pufferfish in pieces and ready for preparation. A keen eye is needed to identify the poisonous organs

Eating fugu: compliments to the chef – if still alive afterwards!

THE RAY'S STING
The venom of a stingray's sting is made in shiny white tissue running along the two grooves on the spine's underside. In the European species the spine is about 12 cm (5 in) long. In larger tropical species it may reach up to 40 cm (16 in).

STING IN THE TAIL
More than 100 species of stingray lurk in coastal shallows around the world. Some grow to great size, with a "wingspan" of more than 3 m (10 ft) and weighing well over 300 kg (660 lb). They tend to hide in the bottom sand and sediment, or glide along slowly as they search for shellfish and fish to crack and crush with their rows of blunt teeth. When in trouble, these rays bring the sting in their tail into play. Some stingrays have two or even three stings. Under threat, the ray lashes its tail to and fro or even arches it over its head, slashing with its sting and stabbing it into the enemy.

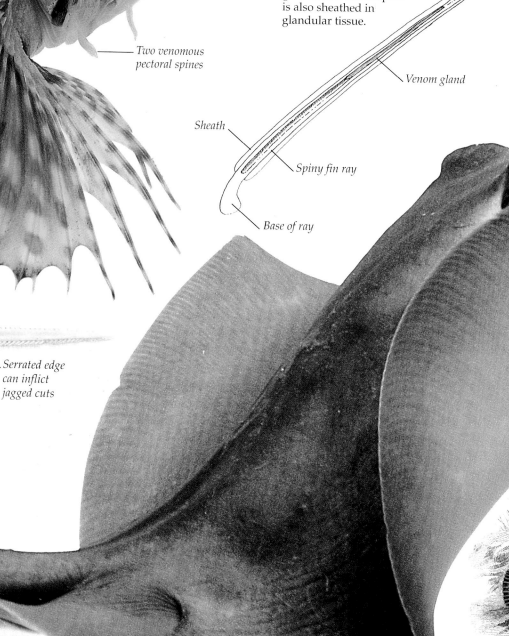

DEADLY BEAUTY

Lionfish, scorpionfish, zebrafish, dragonfish, turkeyfish, firefish – call it what you will – this creature is one of the most poisonous in the sea. The spiny rays in its decorative, lacy fins house glands which make a powerful venom which can disable predators, and has been reported as fatal to humans. The lionfish grows up to 40 cm (16 in) long and swims in shallow waters around reefs and rocks, in warm regions from the Red Sea across the Indian Ocean to the Pacific. For much of the time it swims lazily along, able to ignore predators because its red-brown stripy body is one of nature's warning patterns. If the lionfish spots a small fish or shellfish that looks a likely prey, it can dart forwards and strike with lightning speed.

Thirteen venomous dorsal spines

Eye

Two venomous pectoral spines

Serrated edge can inflict jagged cuts

IN THE GROOVE

Each lionfish spine bears a venom gland lying in a long central groove. The entire spine is also sheathed in glandular tissue.

Venom gland

Sheath

Spiny fin ray

Base of ray

STONY FACED

The stonefish belongs to the scorpionfish family. Its warty body blends perfectly into the stony sea bed, and weeds and anemones grow on it to aid camouflage. In defence, the fish raises the spines along its back. These can inject the most potent of all fish venoms; even a single sting can kill.

Eye of stingray

Large pectoral fin

BE WARY OF THE WEEVER

The lesser weever, or viperfish, lies partly buried in sand, waiting for its food of small shellfish, crabs, and fish. If molested, or stepped upon unwittingly, defensive venom flows from glands at the base of the erected, grooved spines on the gill covers and first dorsal fin.

Escaping the cold

MANY ANIMALS ARE at their most vulnerable during the winter months. Cold temperatures, lack of food, drought, overpopulation, and other problems are best avoided with one of two options – by leaving the area, or by sleeping through the long winter season. Some fast-travelling creatures, such as birds, butterflies, and whales, go on annual long-distance migrations which tie in with the cycle of the seasons. Shorter-lived or slower-moving species such as herds of gazelle or bison may travel in a more haphazard fashion, depending on local conditions. Or they migrate in one direction, breed away from their original area, and then let their offspring make the return journey by themselves. The second option is to stay put but find a sheltered, safe place and go into a deep sleep, called hibernation. This maximizes the animal's chances of survival by saving its energy, as well as making it less conspicuous to hungry predators.

SLIPSTREAM
Flying in a V-shaped formation, like these snow geese, helps birds to save energy on a long journey. The birds following the leader fly in the "slipstream" of the bird in front. When the leader tires, another bird takes over.

SHORT SUMMER
The red-breasted goose is one of many birds that migrate to the Arctic tundra to nest in the brief summer when there is plenty of food available. As the northern winter closes in, it flies more than a thousand kilometres south to less harsh conditions.

UP NORTH
The cloudless sulphur is a fairly large, strong-flying butterfly. In spring, large numbers of cloudless sulphurs migrate from southern North America to more northerly areas.

MIGRATING MAMMAL
The grey whale is a famous migrator of the Pacific Ocean. In the winter months, grey whales spend their time in the warm waters off Baja California and nearby areas, where the mothers give birth to their calves in the calm coastal seas. In spring, the whales move north, following the coastline. They head for the waters off Alaska, where there is a summer flush of food, with long hours of daylight and plentiful nutrients brought by ocean currents. In the autumn they head back south again. Some individuals swim up to 20,000 km (12,500 miles) on the yearly round trip.

DOWN MEXICO WAY
Monarchs are big, powerful butterflies. As summer draws to a close, they travel from Canada and eastern USA to their warmer wintering sites in the southern USA and Mexico. Here they rest in their millions on trees and rocks. As spring arrives they head up north again, to breed and continue the yearly cycle.

CAR TROUBLE
The African migrant butterfly often travels in huge swarms. Local migrations in large numbers may occur anywhere over Africa south of the Sahara. Cars driven through swarms sometimes overheat because their radiators become clogged with dead butterflies.

SILVER-Y
The silver-Y moth often journeys north from Africa and southern Europe, but the details of its travels have not been studied in depth. It cannot survive the winters in northern Europe, but moths that have survived further south breed, and the next generation then moves north. Some fly directly to northern Europe, and others may stop and breed on the way.

BOGONG PITSTOP
The Australian bogong moth can cover buildings in Canberrra, Australia, as it rests during its migration. The moths fly to caves in the Australian Alps at about 1,500 m (5,000 ft) where they spend the hot dry months. They move north again in the cooler autumn.

LONGHAUL LADY
The painted lady is one of the most widespread of all butterflies. It is a strong flier, and individuals can travel up to 1,000 km (620 miles). In Europe, for example, it moves northwards each spring, until the adults are killed off by cold weather.

Hibernation
Only warm-blooded animals – mammals and birds – are true hibernators. Hibernation is not just a long sleep. The animal's body temperature falls from 30-40°C down to perhaps 5°C. Its heart (pulse) rate drops to once every minute or less, and it may breathe only once every half hour. This extra-deep sleep state saves huge amounts of energy, so the hibernator can survive on food reserves stored as body fats for months on end. When a cold-blooded animal becomes so cool that it cannot move and seems to be sleeping, this is called torpor.

HIBERNATING BEAR
Unlike many mammals, bears do not undergo true hibernation. Instead, a bear sleeps very deeply in winter. Its body temperature drops, and its heartbeat slows down. In this way it saves energy, yet it can rouse itself in mild winter weather and go out searching for food.

SAFE SLEEP
During the warm season, bats use great amounts of energy to fuel their small, warm-blooded body for active flight. In the cold season, when their insect prey is absent, they have little option but to hibernate. Bats like this noctule may migrate hundreds of kilometres to a suitable frost-free cave for winter hibernation.

VARIATION
Variation among the individuals of a species is
the raw material on which evolution works. These
butterflies are all the same species – the small copper.
But they differ in coloration, which may help some
individuals. For example, the darker ones warm up
quicker in the sun, so in a cool summer they may
survive better than the lighter ones.
The differences may be
inherited by their
offspring.

CHAPTER 5

EVOLUTION & EXTINCTION

WE LIVE IN A changing world. Nature is altering too, and has been for millions of years. The change in living things through time is called evolution. It happens mainly in response to the changing conditions here on Earth. Climates fluctuate, ice ages come and go, and long droughts are followed by wet periods. Over millions of years, new kinds of plants and animals appear, which are better suited to the new conditions. Other animals and plants are less successful. They die out and become extinct, disappearing forever.

FOSSILS
Much of the evidence for the evolution of life comes from fossils. These are the remains of animals and plants from long ago, which have been preserved in the rocks and turned to stone. Usually only the hard parts are fossilized, such as bones, teeth, horns, claws, and shells. This is the fossil skeleton of a giant rhino, *Arsinoitherium*, which lived about 30 million years ago in Egypt. By comparing its bones with those of animals today, palaeontologists (fossil experts) can make good guesses about its appearance and lifestyle.

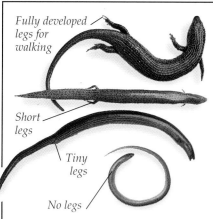

Fully developed legs for walking

Short legs

Tiny legs

No legs

SKINKS LOSING LEGS
These skinks chart every stage in the evolution that led from a normal lizard to a legless one, showing how snakes may have evolved from a legged, reptile ancestor. The first stage may have involved the legs shrinking and being used only for running. Some skinks can choose to move like a snake. They straighten their legs and hold them against their body. They can then wriggle through long grass or into a crack in a rock.

Changing for the better

THE WAY IN WHICH an animal or plant fits into its surroundings is called adaptation. The better adapted it is to the environment, the more likely it is to survive and reproduce. "Environment" here means not only physical conditions such as temperature, light, and availability of shelter. It also means that biological conditions such as food, predators, competitors, and rivals for mates. Examples of how animals are adapted to their environment are everywhere in nature, from a tiger's stripy camouflage to a fish's gills. Every detail of an animal's body and behaviour is shaped by nature. It has evolved to maximize the chances of survival. But the environment, both physical and biological, is never constant. Other animals are always evolving and adapting to improve their own chances, which means the food sources of carnivorous creatures change. Plants evolve to suit their surroundings and withstand being eaten, which means the food sources of herbivorous animals are also changing. And so continues a never-ending struggle to avoid extinction.

Left foot forward

Tail curves to right

Front right foot forward

Front left foot forward

PAST, PRESENT, AND FUTURE
The tiger salamander from North America is the largest of the land-living salamanders. It grows up to 40 cm (16 in) long, and feeds on worms, insects, small mammals such as mice, and some of its amphibian relations such as little frogs. As the salamander walks along, its body bends from side to side in S-shaped curves. This basic method of moving was inherited millions of years ago from the ancestors of the amphibians – fish. The same major feature has been passed along an evolutionary sequence, and been adapted to each animal's needs, according to its habits and lifestyle.

Tail curves to right

Walking sequence of tiger salamander

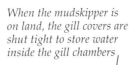

Body curves left

When the mudskipper is on land, the gill covers are shut tight to store water inside the gill chambers

Nostrils are called nares

Mouth is shaped for snapping up insects, spiders, and even small crabs

Sharp teeth for grabbing prey

SECONDARY ADAPTATION

The first fish evolved about 500 million years ago. To breathe, they developed feathery gills to extract oxygen from the water. The mudskipper has evolved a further adaptation. This small fish lives on muddy shores and estuaries around the warm shores of the Indian and Pacific Oceans. One problem with this habitat is that the retreating tide may trap it in a small pool. So the mudskipper holds a quantity of water in its large gill chambers, and "breathes" the oxygen in this, as it skitters across the mud in the open air, to find a better pool. Mudskippers have refined this process so that they can also absorb oxygen directly from the air, through the blood-rich skin lining the back of the mouth and throat. This means that they can stay out of water for longer.

Natural selection

EVOLUTION IS THE ADAPTATION of an animal or plant to its surroundings. In animals this usually happens when parents have more offspring that can survive. These offspring are not all the same, but vary in small details of, for example, colour, size, tooth shape, and so on. In the struggle for survival, some variations may help more than others. The animals with these variations have a better chance of living to adulthood and producing their own offspring. If the helpful features are inherited, the offspring also have a better chance of surviving, and in turn passing them down the hereditary line. This process is called evolution by natural selection.

LIVING FOSSIL
The tuatara is a lizard-like reptile that lives only on a few small islands off the coast of New Zealand. It is the sole surviving species of a group of reptiles that flourished millions of years ago. The other members are now extinct, but the tuatara lives on. It seems to be well adapted to its island habitat. And other animals, which might win the battle for natural selection, have not been able to reach the islands because of their isolation.

CREATURE FEATURES
This colourful cricket from South America has very long, powerful back legs for jumping, and large wings. When disturbed by a predator it can leap into the air and fly away. But if its legs and wings had been even bigger, so as to escape even faster, the cricket would be impaired rather than assisted. Its body parts would be too heavy to move effectively, and use up too much energy when working, or be too obvious when the cricket was trying to hide. Each feature of a creature is a compromise. It has to fulfil many different functions, some of which may not be obvious.

Large muscles to propel back legs

Green wings provide effective camouflage

SWIFT SHAPES

The lesser spotted dogfish is a small type of shark. Its sleek body shape enables it to move swiftly through the water in S-shaped body curves (left). This overall body shape has also evolved in other hunting fish which are only distantly related to the dogfish, as well as other aquatic animals, such as dolphins. When natural selection comes up with the same solution in unrelated groups of animals, this is called convergent evolution.

THOROUGHLY MODERN TEETH

These sharks' teeth from millions of years ago have been turned to stone as fossils. They are remarkably similar to the teeth of sharks today. In their shape, and the shape of the whole shark, nature came up with a successful design very early on in evolution. The details have altered as sharks have adapted to slightly different habitats, but the overall plan has hardly changed in well over 300 million years. Natural selection has yet to come up with any improvements.

Root

Cutting edge

Fossilized
sharks' teeth

JAW SELECTION

The Nile crocodile lurks unseen in the water, then lunges forward with an amazing burst of speed to grab a drinking animal. The crocodile drags its victim under the surface and holds it there until it drowns. This great reptile grows to over 5 metres long, and its massive jaws may be almost 1 metre in length. But even larger jaws would be pointless, because the muscles needed to close such huge jaws would use up lots of energy, and the crocodile's head would be too big to lunge at prey.

Species and their origins

THE SPECIES IS THE BASIC GROUP or "unit" of animals (or plants) in nature. Members of a species can breed successfully with each other, but not with members of other species. Evolution is basically the appearance of new species and the extinction of others. In general, most new species arise when a group from one species becomes cut off from the rest of its kind, especially if it then lives in conditions that differ from those of the parent species. This might happen, for example, when birds are blown off course and reach distant islands or cross a mountain range. Sheer distance can also be a physical barrier. Under new conditions, natural selection means that the isolated group begins to develop new adaptations. It may develop into a new race or subspecies. In time, that subspecies can change so much and become so different from the rest of its species that the two can no longer interbreed. Once this happens, they are two distinct species.

THE COMTE DE BUFFON
Georges Buffon (1707-1788) of France was the first to define a species as a group of living things that can all potentially interbreed with each other, but not with members of other species.

Herring gull
(*Larus argentatus argentatus*)

Lesser black-backed gull (*Larus fuscus graellsii*)

ONE SPECIES OR TWO?
The herring gull (left) and the lesser black-backed gull (right) are descended from gulls that lived in eastern Siberia. These ancestral gulls spread out to both east and west. In time, the two lines of migration met on the other side of the globe, over Europe. The two ends of this circle are the herring gull and the lesser black-backed gull, which have changed so much that they rarely interbreed.

RING SPECIES
Each of the different subspecies of herring gull interbreeds with its neighbours, as do the different subspecies of lesser black-backed gull. In eastern Siberia, the herring gulls interbreed with neighbours that are called black-backed gulls, but could just as well be called herring gulls. These gulls form a "ring species" and show how new species can arise through accumulated small changes.

Larus argentatus vegae

Larus argentatus birulaii

Larus fuscus antellus

Larus fuscus heuglini

Larus argentatus omissus

Larus argentatus smithsonianus

Larus argentatus argentatus

Larus fuscus fuscus

Larus fuscus graellsii

Staying separate

A new species may develop in isolation, but then moves back to where the parent species lives. The two species may mate and produce young, which are infertile. Producing such offspring is a waste of energy for the parents, so they have learnt to recognize their own species using smell, sound, colour, or behaviour. These signals, which keep species apart, are called "isolating mechanisms".

Chiff-chaff · Wood warbler · Willow warbler

NOT ONE, BUT THREE
The English naturalist Gilbert White (1720-1793) was the first to notice that the chiff-chaff, the willow warbler, and the wood warbler were three different species, and not just one. Apart from very slight physical variations, their songs are all distinctly different. For the birds, the songs are used by the female to select a mate, so in this way they act as an isolating mechanism, separating the otherwise similar species.

Froglets set off into the wide world

THE NUMBERS GAME
A frog can lay hundreds of eggs in a single year. If all these survived to adulthood and produced young of their own, the world would be knee-deep in frogs within 10 years. Clearly, most of them die. Many of the deaths are due to chance. But any small advantage, inherited from the parents, will assist the struggle for survival. Over many generations, it will gradually become more common until all members of the species have it.

PERFUMED PARTNERS
Mice, voles, and many other mammals look similar, but they can recognize their own species by characteristic scents. These are used to confirm that the correct choice of partner has been made.

Adult frog

The evolution of fish

FISHY LANDSCAPE
The first fish with jaws appeared 435 million years ago, during the Silurian period. This weird scene shows where they might have swum.

NEARLY 500 MILLION YEARS AGO, the first fish swam in the Earth's waters. They had no jaws, fins, or scales like the fish of today. But early fish did have a type of backbone (the feature that divides the animal kingdom into two groups, the vertebrates and the backbone-less invertebrates). The backbone formed a firm yet flexible central brace against which muscles could pull, to propel the creature along. Fish were also the first creatures to develop jaws. This was a major advance since jaws allowed these fish to bite and chew on items that were too large to swallow in a single gulp. They were a great success. Today, all fish except the lampreys and hagfish have jaws of some kind.

TINY SPINY
Ischnacanthus was an acanthodian or "spiny shark". These ancient fish, although not true sharks, were somewhat shark-like in shape, and each fin had a strong spine along its front edge. They flourished about 400-350 million years ago and then gradually died out.

JAWLESS WONDER
Cephalaspis belonged to a group of jawless extinct fish called osteostracans, which were among the first fish to appear on Earth. This fossil is nearly 400 million years old. The large, bony shield protected the fish's head and gills.

FIRST OF THE RAY-FINS
The palaeonisciforms were the first of the bony, "ray-finned" fish which now include the teleosts. At first the rod-like fin rays (lepidotrichs) were parallel to the fish's body, but gradually they splayed out to make a fan shape as in the fins of most modern fish. In this fine fossil of *Palaeoniscus* (below), from 250 million years ago, the sculpted individual body scales are clearly visible.

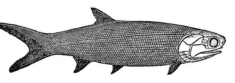

Restoration of *Palaeoniscus*

Cartilage struts

Sculpted individual body scales

Scales

ROUNDED HOLOSTEAN
Dapedium dates from the Lower Jurassic period, some 190 million years ago. It was a holostean, a member of a group that was common at this time. Holosteans had a fully developed backbone, but the rest of the bony skeleton was poorly developed. Today there are still some living species of holosteans, including the gars of North and Central America.

Large predatory mouth

THE RISE OF THE TELEOSTS
Eurypholis has the streamlined shape, large mouth, and sharp teeth of a hunter. It is a teleost, or "true" bony fish. Teleosts make up the great majority of fish species alive today. These agile and adaptable creatures rose to success some 200-100 million years ago.

This restoration of *Eusthenopteron* shows the bones of the head and internal skeleton

ALMOST THERE
Teleost fish such as the small *Stichocentrus* gradually took over the waters from the many fish groups that had gone before. With their bony inner skeletons, flexible fins, efficient jaws, and lightweight scales, they had come a long way from the jawless, heavily armoured tank-like versions such as *Cephalaspis*.

FINS TO LEGS
The slim, predatory *Eusthenopteron* was a primitive lobe-finned fish. The base of each fin had a fleshy, muscular lobe, outwardly resembling a leg. Fish like this may have evolved into amphibians. However, *Eusthenopteron* itself was not an amphibian ancestor, but merely a "fish" adapted to the conditions of its time.

STRUT-FILLED WINGS
Rays have skeletons made of cartilage, which is softer and decays more quickly than bone, so it is fossilized less often. Therefore we know less about the evolution of rays and sharks, compared to bony fish. This specimen, *Heliobatis*, which is a kind of stingray, displays the many cartilage struts in its "wings", or pectoral fins.

Flipper-like fins

Famous fish

In 1938 scientists were startled by the discovery in South Africa of a lobe-fin fish called the coelacanth. Many fossil coelacanths were known, dating back to nearly 400 million years ago. Experts had thought they had died out 80 million years ago, but it seemed local people had been catching them for years. They are "living fossils", survivors from prehistory. More than 100 coelacanths have since been caught, and some have been filmed swimming in the sea near the Comoro Islands, off southeast Africa.

The coelacanth today – still alive and swimming

Ancient amphibians

THE FIRST AMPHIBIANS appeared some 360 million years ago. They evolved from fish with fleshy, lobed fins which looked like legs, and the earliest amphibians such as *Ichthyostega* still had fish-like features. They may have been attracted on to land by a good supply of food and fewer enemies to prey on them. While their fish ancestors already had lungs for breathing air and had begun to use their lobed fins for moving around on land, the early amphibians developed efficient walking limbs. The Great Age of amphibians was from the Devonian to the Permian periods. Most amphibians had become extinct by the Triassic period, leaving only a few, such as *Triadobatrachus*, to evolve into modern amphibians.

Artist's reconstruction of *Triadobatrachus*

One half of *Triadobatrachus* fossil

Skeleton of *Ichthyostega*

Reconstruction of *Ichthyostega*

FISHY FINS
These are reconstructions of *Ichthyostega*, an early amphibian from the Devonian period in Greenland. It had some fish-like features such as a tail fin and small scales in its distinctly amphibian body, but had fewer skull bones and legs suitable for walking.

AMPHIBIAN CROCODILE
This skeleton is of *Eryops*, a crocodile-like amphibian which lived in swamps in Texas in the southern USA about 250 million years ago. These terrestrial creatures used their strong limbs to move around on land.

Scales

ROUNDED HOLOSTEAN

Dapedium dates from the Lower Jurassic period, some 190 million years ago. It was a holostean, a member of a group that was common at this time. Holosteans had a fully developed backbone, but the rest of the bony skeleton was poorly developed. Today there are still some living species of holosteans, including the gars of North and Central America.

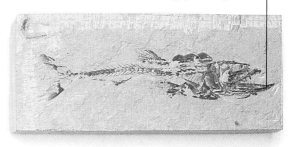

Large predatory mouth

THE RISE OF THE TELEOSTS

Eurypholis has the streamlined shape, large mouth, and sharp teeth of a hunter. It is a teleost, or "true" bony fish. Teleosts make up the great majority of fish species alive today. These agile and adaptable creatures rose to success some 200-100 million years ago.

This restoration of *Eusthenopteron* shows the bones of the head and internal skeleton

FINS TO LEGS

The slim, predatory *Eusthenopteron* was a primitive lobe-finned fish. The base of each fin had a fleshy, muscular lobe, outwardly resembling a leg. Fish like this may have evolved into amphibians. However, *Eusthenopteron* itself was not an amphibian ancestor, but merely a "fish" adapted to the conditions of its time.

ALMOST THERE

Teleost fish such as the small *Stichocentrus* gradually took over the waters from the many fish groups that had gone before. With their bony inner skeletons, flexible fins, efficient jaws, and lightweight scales, they had come a long way from the jawless, heavily armoured tank-like versions such as *Cephalaspis*.

STRUT-FILLED WINGS

Rays have skeletons made of cartilage, which is softer and decays more quickly than bone, so it is fossilized less often. Therefore we know less about the evolution of rays and sharks, compared to bony fish. This specimen, *Heliobatis*, which is a kind of stingray, displays the many cartilage struts in its "wings", or pectoral fins.

Flipper-like fins

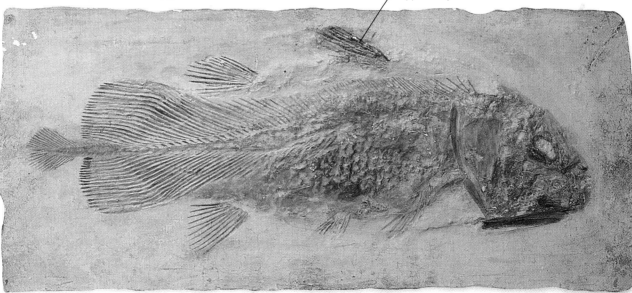

Famous fish

In 1938 scientists were startled by the discovery in South Africa of a lobe-fin fish called the coelacanth. Many fossil coelacanths were known, dating back to nearly 400 million years ago. Experts had thought they had died out 80 million years ago, but it seemed local people had been catching them for years. They are "living fossils", survivors from prehistory. More than 100 coelacanths have since been caught, and some have been filmed swimming in the sea near the Comoro Islands, off southeast Africa.

The coelacanth today – still alive and swimming

First on land

ANIMALS HAD NO REASON to venture on land until there were plants there for food and shelter. The first plants had gained a roothold on land at the start of the Devonian period, almost 400 million years ago. They were soon followed by the first land animals, which probably resembled millipedes, centipedes, and scorpions, and then wingless insects. The first winged insects flew through the coal forests that covered the Earth over 300 million years ago. Early fossil remains show that a few of these insects, such as dragonflies and cockroaches, would have looked very similar to present-day species. But others represent groups that are no longer alive today. Because insects are usually small and delicate, most of them probably rotted away before they could become trapped in muddy sediments, or amber, and fossilized. And so, with very little fossil evidence, no one is yet sure how insects evolved.

INSECT JEWELLERY
Amber has been looked on as precious stone for centuries. This piece of Baltic amber, cut and polished as a pendant, contains three quite different types of fly.

Limestone fossil of a moth's wing from southern England

SHOW YOUR COLOURS
Pigments in the scales of this fossilized wing have altered the process of fossilization, so that parts of the pattern can still be seen millions of years later.

LIVING ANCESTORS?
The peripatus, or velvet worm, may represent a stage between worms and insects. It has a worm's soft, segmented body, but clawed legs like an insect and a similar heart and breathing system.

SPRINGTAILS
The wingless springtail is very similar to the first insects to evolve. Many springtails have a curious forked jumping organ folded up under their tail – hence the name. This species, on the underside of a dead limpet, lives on the seashore.

Modern-day "sweat bee" (*Trigona* species)

How amber is formed

Amber is the fossil resin of pine trees from millions of years ago. As the resin oozed from cracks in the tree trunks, creatures attracted by the sweet scent became trapped on its sticky surface. In time the resin, including the trapped creatures, hardened and was buried in the soil, and eventually washed into the sea. Copal looks similar to amber but is much younger.

Wing

Delicate legs

EARLY CRANES
About 35 million years ago in what is now Colorado, USA, this crane fly became trapped in muddy sediment at the bottom of a lake or pond. The sediment was so fine that, when it turned to stone, even details of the wings and legs were preserved. This fossilized specimen looks very similar to modern crane flies. The weak, drifting flight and the long, floppy legs were clearly important adaptations to life long before the American continent took its present shape.

BEE IN COPAL
This piece of copal from Zanzibar (an island off the east coast of Africa) could be 1,000 to 1 million years old. It has been magnified to show the beautifully preserved "sweat bee", which looks like the present-day bee.

A STICKY END
Crawling and flying insects, attracted by the pine resin oozing from this tree trunk, are trapped for ever. Scenes like this took place over 40 million years ago.

OLDEST DRAGONFLY

This fossilized folded wing is the oldest known dragonfly. It was found above a coal seam at Bolsover Colliery in Derbyshire, England, 700 m (2,300 ft) underground. The dragonfly flew 300 million years ago and had a total wing span of 20 cm (8 in) – considerably larger than the largest present-day species shown here.

Broken wing

FLOWERING PLANTS

The appearance of the first flowering plants, about 130 million years ago, signified a new source of food in the form of pollen and nectar. Insects thrived on this new food, and the flowering plants thrived because of the variety of pollinating insects. The number of insects and plants increased together, a process called coevolution.

LARGEST DRAGONFLY

This dragonfly (*Tetracanthagyna plagiata*) from Borneo is a member of the largest dragonfly species still in existence today. The largest dragonfly ever known is a fossilized specimen from the USA, with a wing span of about 60 cm (24 in) – over three times that of today's record holder.

Compound eye

Black spot, or stigma

Wings and legs attached to thorax

Veins

Unlike the wings of more recently developed insects, dragonfly wings do not fold

Abdomen

DRAGONFLY PREDATORS

The artist of this whimsical engraving clearly had more imagination than biological knowledge. Present-day dragonflies are fast and skilled fliers. Fossils prove their ancestors were similar and would not have made easy prey for a pterosaur.

Present-day earwig

DROWNED EARWIG

The lake deposits at Florissant, Colorado, USA, are about 35 million years old. They contain many well-preserved insect fossils because of the fine sediment from which the rocks were formed.

Tip of abdomen

Veins on wings

TURNED TO STONE

Fossilized specimens of smaller dragonfly species, such as this one from southern England, are relatively common. Even though this specimen appears to be missing a wing, it is possible to see all the veins quite clearly.

Ancient amphibians

THE FIRST AMPHIBIANS appeared some 360 million years ago. They evolved from fish with fleshy, lobed fins which looked like legs, and the earliest amphibians such as *Ichthyostega* still had fish-like features. They may have been attracted on to land by a good supply of food and fewer enemies to prey on them. While their fish ancestors already had lungs for breathing air and had begun to use their lobed fins for moving around on land, the early amphibians developed efficient walking limbs. The Great Age of amphibians was from the Devonian to the Permian periods. Most amphibians had become extinct by the Triassic period, leaving only a few, such as *Triadobatrachus*, to evolve into modern amphibians.

Artist's reconstruction of *Triadobatrachus*

Skeleton of *Ichthyostega*

Reconstruction of *Ichthyostega*

One half of *Triadobatrachus* fossil

FISHY FINS
These are reconstructions of *Ichthyostega,* an early amphibian from the Devonian period in Greenland. It had some fish-like features such as a tail fin and small scales in its distinctly amphibian body, but had fewer skull bones and legs suitable for walking.

AMPHIBIAN CROCODILE
This skeleton is of *Eryops,* a crocodile-like amphibian which lived in swamps in Texas in the southern USA about 250 million years ago. These terrestrial creatures used their strong limbs to move around on land.

Wide, flat skull,
like modern frog

Short tail

ANCIENT FROG
This 20 million-year-old fossil frog, *Discoglossus*, was
found in Germany. It is structurally similar to its
close relative from 130 million years previously,
Eodiscoglossus, which was found in Spain. The
modern living species of *Discoglossus* show that
they have remained almost unchanged over the
last 150 million years. This is a fine example of
what is known as conservative evolution.

Outline
of fossil frog

**SLIM
EVIDENCE**
This fossil sandwich,
which was found in
France, is the only known
specimen of *Triadobatrachus*,
dating from the Triassic
period about 210 million
years ago. It has a frog-
like body and skull, but
it is different enough from
true frogs to be placed in
a separate group called
the proanurans.

MORE MODERN FROG
Well-preserved fossil frog skeletons like *Rana pueyoi*
from the Miocene of Spain, are very like the modern
European frogs which belong to the same genus,
Rana. Fossil frogs like this help experts to date when
modern frog groups first appeared. They also show
how little some groups have changed in the last
25 million years since the early Miocene period.

Fleshy, long hind legs

Body shape
of fossil
salamander
is like that of
modern
hellbender

Short, stout leg
supports heavy body

Diplocaulus lived
270 million years ago

RELATIVE FROM ABROAD
This fossil salamander,
Cryptobranchus, was found in
Switzerland and is about eight
million years old. It is a close relative
of the hellbenders; the only living
one, *Cryptobranchus alleganiensis*,
is found in the southeastern USA.
Fossils like this show that some
amphibians, such as these
hellbenders, once had a wider
distribution, and that separate
land masses were once joined.

The Age of Reptiles

THE FIRST REPTILES were probably small, lizard-like creatures which evolved from amphibians more than 330 million years ago. They lived alongside the giant land-based amphibians for millions of years. But by 200 million years ago, reptiles had diversified into several different groups. Turtles, tortoises, crocodiles, and lizards, were all very similar to their representatives today. Another group that was spreading and evolving rapidly was the dinosaurs. These incredibly varied and successful reptiles dominated life on land for over 120 million years. Some, like the giraffe-necked *Brachiosaurus*, weighed over 60 tonnes and stood as tall as a five-storey building. Others were as small as a blackbird. The dinosaurs shown here belonged to the stegosaur or "roofed reptile" group, which thrived around 150 million years ago. *Stegosaurus* lived in North America and *Tuojiangosaurus* (the large skeleton) lived in what is now China.

CAUGHT IN THE RAIN
Stegosaurus, shown here caught in a downpour, probably had two rows of large upright plates in two parallel rows down its back. The plates were made of bone with honeycomb-like spaces running through – not much use as defensive armour plating.

A WEIRD STEGOSAUR
This etching shows an early attempt to reconstruct a plated dinosaur, with hedgehog-like spines instead of bony plates! It is unlikely that stegosaurs would have walked on two legs. Their front feet were adapted purely for walking.

Vertebral spine

Cone-shaped plate

Bony flange to anchor tail-swinging muscle

Heavy tail counterbalances weight of head and body

Part of hipbone (pelvis)

Chevron bone

Broad, flat feet

SPIKY TAIL
The large, cone-shaped plates on the back of *Tuojiangosaurus* give way to two pairs of sharply pointed ones, which were used as lethal weapons. Stegosaurs could swing their muscular tails from side to side with great force. The tail muscles were anchored to the bony flanges above and below each backbone (vertebra).

Sharp defensive spike

WARMING UP

Dimetrodon was an early reptile that lived before the dinosaurs. It used the large sail on its back to absorb the heat of the sun on cool days, and so warm its body. Some plated dinosaurs may have done the same.

Some stegosaurs may have warmed themselves up by basking in the sun – an early use of solar power

Stegosaurus plate, shown at just over half its real size

HOT PLATE

This is one of the smaller plates from the neck region of *Stegosaurus*. These large, flat bones acted like the sail of *Dimetrodon* (above left) to warm or cool the animal. The plates were richly supplied with blood, and *Stegosaurus* would have used this blood like water in a central heating system. Standing in the breeze cooled the blood, while basking in the sun raised the body temperature.

Large plates of bone on back

Shoulder blade (scapula)

Cervical (neck) ribs

Skeleton of the Chinese stegosaur, *Tuojiangosaurus*

Rib

POORLY DEFENDED

Like all stegosaurs, *Tuojiangosaurus'* flanks and belly were vulnerable to attack. The spikes in the tail were the main weapon used to fend off attacks of large meat-eating dinosaurs.

Long hind limbs

Head stays close to the ground to feed on low-growing vegetation

Short front limbs

A QUESTION OF SIZE

Stegosaurs were not really that big. Unlike this man (right), an adult would have stood as tall as the plates on *Tuojiangosaurus'* back.

PEA BRAIN

Stegosaurs are famous for having tiny brains in proportion to their size. *Stegosaurus* had a brain the size of a walnut. This has given some people the idea that dinosaurs were stupid or slow. But stegosaurs' brains were obviously ample for their needs, as they managed to survive for over 10 million years.

Dinosaur diets

IT IS EASY TO IMAGINE DINOSAURS as being fearsome, meat-eating creatures. But some were peaceful plant eaters that simply browsed amongst the treetops, tearing off leaves. Other dinosaurs ate a mixed diet of meat and plants. Those that were not vegetarian did not confine themselves to dinosaur meat. They would have eaten anything that moved, including insects and birds. Fossilized dinosaur remains can tell us a lot about what the animal ate when it was alive. Scientists can compare their jaws and teeth with those of animals alive today, from horses to lions, to find similarities in structure and function. This is called comparative anatomy. Large claws on the fingers and toes show that the dinosaur was a predator; hard plates of body armour, as in *Ankylosaurus*, suggest a slow-moving plant eater.

BY THE RIVER
This scene from 190 million years ago shows meat-eating dinosaurs, swimming reptiles, and flying pterosaurs sharing the same landscape.

TIME FOR DINNER
This carnivorous dinosaur is rearing over its prey, a well-armoured ankylosaur.

Orbit (eye socket)

Weak lower jaw

Pencil-like teeth

Diplodocus skull

SERIOUS TEETH

The fearsome rows of curved, serrated teeth in the *Allosaurus* skull (below) are typical of carnivores. *Allosaurus* may well have fed on the young of herbivores such as *Diplodocus* (opposite). An adult *Diplodocus* would have been too big to tackle, unless *Allosaurus* hunted in packs.

Large cavity helped to reduce weight of skull

Orbit (Eye socket)

Allosaurus skull

VEGETARIAN SKULL

This skull belonged to a huge herbivore called *Diplodocus*. All of the thin, pencil-like teeth are at the front of the mouth. *Diplodocus* would have used them like a rake to draw in conifer needles and leaves. Unable to chew, *Diplodocus* simply swallowed what it raked in.

Powerful lower jaw

Diplodocus

Fern leaf

Massospondylus skull (below)

DIPLODOCUS DINNER

Diplodocus may have raked in plants like this fern leaf. Because it never chewed, it did not need a strong lower jaw.

DUAL DIET DINOSAUR

The skull above belonged to *Massospondylus*. Its teeth, being neither serrated and stabbing, nor rake-like or grinding, were multi-purpose. Small and coarse-edged, they could chew either meat or plants. Animals who can eat like this are called omnivores.

Death of the dinosaurs

DINOSAURS DISAPPEARED from the Earth quite suddenly, and why this happened is still a mystery. Around 70 million years ago, the dinosaurs ruled the Earth. Yet about five million years later, they had all died out, perhaps only in a matter of months. Scientists have various theories to explain their sudden extinction, but many ignore one vital point: dinosaurs were only one of a whole range of creatures that died out at the same time, including all the swimming and flying reptiles. So any theory to explain dinosaur extinction must explain the disappearance of these groups as well. Some people think that small mammals ate all the dinosaur eggs. This is very unlikely – for how would it account for the extinction of other species that disappeared at the same time? Others believed that diseases were responsible, affecting only certain groups.

POISONOUS BITE
It has been suggested that the dinosaurs died out because they ate new kinds of poisonous plants, including the deadly nightshade (above), that began to grow on Earth.

Stony meteorite fragment

Fossilized ammonite shell

ROCKS FROM SPACE
A likely reason for the sudden extinction is that a massive meteorite from space collided with the Earth. This would have been catastrophic, causing a huge steam and dust cloud which darkened the Earth for a long time, killing off many plants and the animals that fed on them.

Iron meteorite fragment

A MASS EXTINCTION
Many other creatures died out at the time of the dinosaur extinction. Whatever happened seemed to affect some creatures, while leaving others unscathed. Ammonites, a type of mollusc, became extinct, as did the mosasaurs, plesiosaurs, and ichthyosaurs, groups of meat-eating marine reptiles. Sea crocodiles died out but the river crocodiles survived. The flying reptiles, pterosaurs, disappeared, but birds were unaffected.

Iguanodon ischium (part of hipbone)

Unaffected part of bone

Shaft of ischium bent forward after repair

Section of
hadrosaur backbone

*Vertebral
spine*

**THE BEGINNING
OF THE END**
A *Tyrannosaurus rex* is
shown fleeing in terror
as a meteor hits the Earth.
The impact would have had
an effect rather like that of a
massive nuclear war. Dense black
clouds of dust and soot would have
cut out the sun for months.

A GROWTH
Dinosaurs could contract cancer. This
section of backbone belonged to a hadrosaur,
or "duck-billed" dinosaur that walked upright
on its back legs, and shows a swollen area
which was a cancerous tumour in the bone.

*Part of ischium that
formed hip joint
with thigh bone*

*Swollen area of
tumour growth*

*Point of
fracture*

*Vertebral
body*

*Thickening of
bone around break*

BROKEN BONE
During their reign, dinosaurs were not immune to diseases
and accidents. The *Iguanodon* hip bone (above) shows a
fracture that healed itself during the creature's lifetime.

Mammoths and mastodons

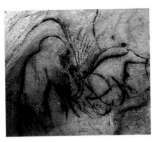

Stone Age painting found in a cave in France

WHEN THE DINOSAURS and many other animals died out, 65 million years ago, they left opportunities for others to take over. The main group which responded very quickly was the mammals. Small, shrew-like mammals had first appeared with the dinosaurs, over 200 million years ago. During the dinosaurs' reign they did not evolve very much, and none was bigger than a pet cat. But by 50 million years ago, all manner of weird and huge mammals walked the Earth, while others took to the water as whales. The elephant group of mammals arose over 40 million years ago. It produced some of the biggest of all land mammals, the mammoths and mastodons. These animals lived until relatively recently alongside Stone Age humans, and some of their bodies have been found deep-frozen in the ice of the far north. We do not know why mammoths and mastodons became extinct, but computer studies of their decline in numbers suggest that it was a combination of overhunting by humans, and changes in the climate that led to their final disappearance 10,000 years ago.

HAIRY LEGS
It is very rare to be able to see the hair, skin, and muscles of long-extinct creatures. Usually only bones and teeth are fossilized, but when frozen mammoths thaw out of the permafrost (permanently frozen ground) in Siberia, we can learn – as with this mammoth leg – about their shaggy coat and long "toenails".

SNOW PLOUGHS
Mammoth tusks curve much more than those of living elephants, and are the biggest teeth of any known creature. Some grew to lengths of 5 m (16 ft). Mothers, as in this reconstruction, would have used them to protect their calves from predators. Mammoths probably also used them to sweep aside snow when feeding on the grassy plains.

Body squashed flat by weight of frozen earth and snow

MAMMOTH TASK
The first whole mammoth to be studied by scientists was found in 1900 beside the River Berezovka in Siberia. A shed was built over the thawing carcass while it was excavated and dissected.

FAST-FROZEN MAMMOTH
Perhaps 40,000 years ago, this baby mammoth died in a Siberian marsh just as the ground froze. In 1977, his frozen body was recovered by scientists, and nicknamed "Dima". One scientist tried to use genes from cells in Dima's best-preserved organs to clone mammoth cells in a test tube. The plan was to implant these cells in a female Asian elephant's womb, in the hope that she would give birth to a bouncing baby mammoth. It did not work.

SIMILAR BUT DIFFERENT
Reconstructions of mammoths and mastodons may look alike, but mastodons differ in several ways from mammoths. Mastodons are stockier, and do not have a steeply sloping back. Some specimens have two small tusks in the lower jaw as well as the big upper tusks.

Mammoths had small ears which helped to reduce loss of body heat in cold conditions

MAMMOTH ANCESTORS
Mammoths evolved in the cold of the frozen north. But their ancestors originated in what is now the Middle East, over 40 million years earlier.

Mammoth stamp from Manama, Bahrain, in the Middle East

IVORY MISSILES
During the Stone Age, ivory was used for making household implements, tools, and weapons. This mammoth-ivory boomerang, found in Poland, dates back 23,000 years. The growth lines in the mammoth's tusk show as cones, one inside the other, along the length of the whole tusk.

A long; woolly coat protected mammoths from freezing temperatures

Reconstruction of an adult female mammoth with her baby at her side

Broad feet spread body weight for walking in soft snow

Adapting to habitats

MOLES HAVE STRONG, BROAD front feet for digging through soil. Ducks have webbed feet for swimming. It is clear that all plants and animals are superbly adapted to their climate and way of life. The English naturalist Charles Darwin (1809-1882) proposed that these adaptations were an outcome of natural selection. Each creature is also adapted to a particular location where conditions suit it best, from a pine wood to a stony desert. These surroundings are called habitats. Some animals, such as the fox, can tolerate a wide range of habitats, from mountains and moors to city parks. It manages this because of its body design and adaptable behaviour. Other creatures need a specialized habitat. The strange, worm-like olm, for example, lives in complete darkness in underground streams and caves in southern Europe, and is highly sensitive to disturbances in the air and water.

PALEY'S WATCH
An English clergyman, William Paley (1743-1805) believed in "natural theology" – a theory that all adaptation was evidence of the Creator's handiwork. He published his ideas in a book which began with the example of himself walking across a heath and finding a watch among the stones. Unlike the stones, the watch had moving parts that worked together for a purpose. Paley said that the existence of the watch proved that there was a watchmaker, so an animal or plant proved the existence of a Creator. By studying natural history, the nature of God could be better understood.

FACE FOR THE HABITAT
Leaf-nosed bats from different habitats have varying face shapes. This may be connected with the difficulty they have in navigating around obstacles, using their sense of echolocation. Bats hunting in woodland must negotiate branches, which bats flying over open water or grassland do not encounter.

Faces of leaf-nosed bats

SUITED FOR THE SOIL
The European mole is well suited for life in the soil. It has tiny eyes, since it rarely uses them; its broad, shovel-like front paws dig through the soil; and its sensitive snout smells and feels for worms, grubs, and other food. Yet this mole would probably not survive underground in a desert or on a moorland. Its habitat is under woodland, meadows, and lawns. Other species of burrowing mammals are better adapted to different habitats.

THE OPEN-WATER HABITAT

With seemingly typical bat behaviour, the Daubenton's bat swoops low over a river or pond, to snatch a meal of flying insects. But in a densely wooded habitat, this bat would have great trouble surviving. This is because its diet, hunting techniques, flying skills, and sound sonar are tuned specifically to its open-water habitat.

Daubenton's bat

STILL CURVED

Modern evolutionary views suggest that humans evolved from chimpanzee-like apes over the past 5-10 million years. From climbing with all four limbs in trees, humans progressed to walking on two legs in more open habitats. The human backbone still retains some of the curvature of its ape ancestry.

Human skull and backbone

WARM INSIDE

The king penguin is superbly adapted for life in the icy water near the South Pole. Its coat of feathers is thick and waterproof and, together with the layer of fatty blubber under the skin, keeps the penguin warm even at temperatures of -30°C (-22°F).

Skeleton of a giant panda's paw

THE PANDA'S THUMB

Bears are carnivores, and their paws have five very short "fingers". Giant pandas, descended from bears, eat bamboo shoots and need a thumb to hold them. They have evolved a thumb, but it is a short imperfect one jutting out from the wrist. It seems that the bear's paw was too specialized for natural selection to "reverse" the basic plan and make a true thumb. Instead, the panda's false thumb grows from a wrist bone.

Thumb

Life in the ocean

LIFE BEGAN IN THE OCEANS millions of years ago. Today, oceans cover 71 per cent of the planet and provide homes for countless animals, including fish, seals, sharks, and jellyfish. Ocean wildlife is at its richest in the warm shallow waters of coral reefs, where dazzlingly colourful fish such as clown triggerfish and angelfish live. In deeper waters, whales, dolphins, and porpoises are found. Most animals live close to the water's surface, where sunlight filters through the water, allowing microscopic plants such as diatoms to flourish. An intricate food web exists here: microscopic animals feed on the diatoms; small animals feed on these; larger sea creatures eat the smaller ones, and all the way up the food chain, to predators such as sharks.

RAY'S WAVES
A ray "flies" through the water by vertical waves that pass along its wing-like pectoral fins, from head to tail.

HUNTING ON THE MARGINS
The black tip reef shark can grow to a length of 2.4 m (8 ft) and lives around the edges of coral reefs. It does not have the slim body and manoeuvrability of fish that usually dwell in the coral reef. Instead, it is streamlined and is adapted for a deep-water lifestyle. This top predator patrols the waters near the reef, taking advantage of the plentiful plant and animal life there by picking off the occasional unwary victim.

MOLLUSC WITH A DIFFERENCE
Like the snail, this squid is a mollusc. It can camouflage itself rapidly, sending waves of colour down its body and squirting out a cloud of dark ink to cover its escape.

SPIDER IN THE FOOD WEB
Crabs, such as this spider crab, tend to inhabit shallow water, where there is sufficient light to encourage plant growth and so feed animal life.

WATER SKATER
Garfish live in shoals in the open ocean. They have beak-like jaws and sharp teeth, and feed on small fish. The garfish escapes predators by vibrating its tail and skittering across the sea's surface, with the front part of its body raised out of the water.

Black tip reef shark

A FUNNY FISH
Bizarre patterns and hues are not only there to look pretty. The clown triggerfish has a dramatic set of broken patterns which breaks up the outline of its body, confusing predators long enough for the fish to get away. The triggerfish takes its name from the second fin spine on its back, which, like a gun's trigger, can lock or release the first spine into an upright position to deter a predator's attack.

Clown triggerfish

INVISIBLE LINKS IN THE CHAIN OF LIFE
The microscopic world of plankton forms the base of the ocean food chain. Phytoplankton, tiny plants such as diatoms and algae, are eaten by zooplankton (magnified above), minuscule animals that drift in the ocean currents. These in turn are eaten by filter feeders from molluscs up to blue whales.

WELL WRAPPED UP
With their streamlined bodies, seals and sea lions are well equipped for life in the ocean. Their oily, glossy fur keeps them warm in cold waters, helped by a thick layer of fat, or blubber, under the skin. Seals use their front flippers like oars as they speed after fish in the sea. There are more than 30 kinds of seals and sea lions in the world, including this grey seal (above).

171

Freshwater habitats

FRESH WATER MAKES UP only three percent of all water on Earth, the rest being salty sea water. But freshwater habitats are more variable than ocean habitats, varying from foaming streams to sluggish rivers, and tiny puddles and pools to vast lakes. The chemical content of the water is often affected by the rock type underneath it. Where there is a rich supply of nutrients, encouraging the growth of plants, there is a large number and variety of animals, such as insect larvae, fish, aquatic mammals, and birds. Water from highland areas is often clear and rich in oxygen, but lacks nutrients and so is poor in aquatic life. The ecology of fresh water is therefore complicated by these different factors. Some animals are able to live in clear fast-flowing rivers, while others need the still, murky waters of a lake.

TAGGED FISH
Fish are caught and tagged with small metal or plastic clips, to study their growth rate, migration, and life spans. Scientists also tag individual fish to determine the size of the population. This can be calculated using a formula based on the frequency with which the tagged fish are recaptured. By regularly weighing and measuring the tagged fish, scientists can see how each one grows over time.

Caddis fly larvae

POSITIVE INDICATORS
In all rivers there is a profusion of small creatures under stones and amongst the plants. Many, such as the caddis fly larva, mayfly nymph, and bloodworm, are the larval form of flying insects. Some of these animals are sensitive to pollution. Scientists can tell if a river is polluted by counting the numbers of each species found. The presence of caddis fly larvae, mayfly nymphs, and water shrimps indicates clean water, so they are called positive indicators.

Water shrimp

Minnows

Mayfly nymphs

MIDDLE WATERS
As a river widens, so bends begin to develop, and patches of silt and mud accumulate. Plants such as the water crowfoot (right) thrive in this less rapid water. Small invertebrates that live among the weeds provide a rich source of food for bottom-feeding minnows.

Rat-tailed maggot

Tubifex worms

NEGATIVE INDICATORS
If a stretch of river supports only such species as rat-tailed maggots, bloodworms, and tubifex worms, this shows that the water is heavily polluted. Other forms of life may not survive because their gills have been clogged up by particles in the water or because they have been unable to tolerate low oxygen levels. The rat-tailed maggot (the larva of a fly) can survive because it takes in air using a specialized breathing tube rather like a snorkel.

Bloodworm

WATER CROWFOOT
Like plants found in streams and rivers, the water crowfoot is adapted to resist the pull of the current. It puts down strong roots in the river bed, and its leaves have long, thin stems, which bend with the flow of the water

Rainbow trout

FASTER WATERS

The upper reaches of a
river are often fast flowing
and well oxygenated, providing
perfect conditions for rainbow trout
and a few other small fish that can cope
with this environment. These creatures are
powerful swimmers, and can cope with the swift
current. They save energy by resting near the edge of the
river or by a boulder, where the water flows more slowly.

SLOWER WATERS

In the lower reaches of the river, the gradient is less steep and the water flows
more slowly. Silt and nutrients tend to settle on the river bed, providing a
foothold for a diversity of plants. These enrich the food supply for other
organisms so the lower reaches contain a variety of fish. Within
this zone, different parts of the river attract different species.
The barbel occupies the clearer,
faster-flowing parts, for
example below weirs.
Tench prefer slower,
muddier water, and
pike live wherever
there is enough
weed to hide
them as they
lie in ambush.

Tench

Barbel

*Barbels for
locating food*

*Flattened underside for
bottom-dwelling lifestyle*

*Powerful tail and
fins for rapid
acceleration*

*Forward-facing
eyes for distance*

*Camouflaged
colouring*

Juvenile pike

The woodland habitat

THE WOODLANDS in temperate regions (between the tropics and the polar circles) provide shelter for a large wildlife community. Every tree supports its own web of life: insects feed on the leaves, birds and mammals nest in the trunk and branches, and woodlice and beetles live in the leaf litter. Seasonal weather changes affect animal behaviour. In the warm spring days insects emerge, birds begin to nest, and young mammals are born. In the hot summer months the young animals grow quickly. Most trees lose their leaves in the autumn, and the animals feast on berries or store food for the winter. The cold nights and short days make winter a difficult time: many animals grow thick coats and spend more time in their burrows or tree holes, while some birds fly away to spend the winter in warmer climates.

GALL STORY
Forest food chains can be complicated. Insects such as moths and wasps lay their eggs in buds, leaves, and fruits, where the larvae develop inside swellings called galls. The chalci wasp searches out the larvae and lays its eggs in them.

GREEN WOODPECKER
The forest food chain continues when, in turn, both the larvae inside the galls and the chalci wasp (above) are eaten by insect-hunting birds such as this green woodpecker.

The short tail is made of stiff feathers which support the woodpecker as it climbs up trees

Canopy: gets full strength of Sun

Litter layer: plants that thrive in moist, shady conditions

Shrub layer: tall bushes and small trees

Herb layer: plants that can cope with low light levels

Topsoil

Subsoil

Bedrock

WOODEN HOSTS
Trees provide a variety of smaller habitats, in vertical layers in the forest. Flying creatures such as birds and butterflies frequent the topmost canopy, where leaves and fruits are profuse. On the forest floor conditions are cool, shady, and damp, which suits worms, snails, and similar small creatures.

NIGHT FLIER
An unmistakable hoot in the night reveals that there is a tawny owl in the woods. During the day, the owl sits quietly amongst the trees. It is hard to spot, because its mottled colouring blends in with the bark and leaves. Its sharp hearing and silent flight make it an excellent hunter of mice, voles, and other small mammals, as well as small birds, amphibians, fish, and insects.

LEAF LITTER CARNIVORE

Centipedes scurry through the leaf litter on the forest floor. They seize small prey such as worms, grubs, and larvae in their large fangs and inject poison to subdue the victim. Centipedes have one pair of legs per body segment; their plant-eating cousins, millipedes, have two pairs.

Fur, feathers, and bones

Vole's skull

Rodent's hip bone

OWL PELLETS

Some birds, such as owls and members of the crow family, bring up the indigestible parts of their food as pellets. The pellet contains bones, teeth, fur, claws, feathers, and other hard parts.

BROWSERS

Deer are typical woodland animals. They browse on the tree leaves at dawn and dusk, and rest in the middle of the day in the deep shade of thickets.

Mountain life

THE MOUNTAIN HABITAT is a harsh one, and the greater the altitude, the harsher it becomes. The temperature falls by about 1°C (1.8°F) for every 150 m (500 ft), the winds blow harder, and the atmosphere becomes thinner and less rich in oxygen. Only insects can survive at the high altitudes of the mountain peaks. They feed on plant spores, pollen, and other insects swept up from the lower plains. Most animals live farther down the slopes in the forests and meadows. Many of these mountain animals have thick fur and large lungs to help them survive the cold, the wind, and the thin air. High-altitude animals, such as pumas, usually move down to the lower slopes and valleys in winter. Others, such as marmots and bears, hibernate during the coldest months.

Thick dense fur is a blue-grey colour

Brush-like tail

WELL WRAPPED UP
The Andes mountains of South America are home to the chinchilla – a mountain mammal with a luxurious fur coat. At one time, wild chinchillas were quite common. Today, they are rare because too many have been hunted for their valuable fur.

ALPINE ZONES
Whatever the climate, the increasing altitude on a mountain creates zones of different habitats. These layers show the changing vegetation in the European Alps. Deciduous woodlands in the foothills give way to coniferous forest, which can tolerate the increasing cold. At 2,600 m (8,500 ft) the alpine meadow is the main vegetation. Between the meadow and the snow at the top lies the alpine tundra, with rocky scree above it.

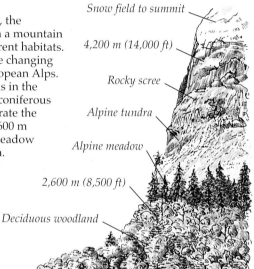

Snow field to summit

4,200 m (14,000 ft)

Rocky scree

Alpine tundra

Alpine meadow

2,600 m (8,500 ft)

Deciduous woodland

BLOOD AND HONEY

Many mountain insects have a varied diet, eating whatever they can find during the different seasons. This fly from the Himalayan region has dual-purpose mouthparts. Its short, strong, biting "jaws" can pierce the skin of mammals such as yaks to feed on the blood, just like the horsefly of meadows and pastures. Its long, thin "tongue" can sip nectar from flowers, when these bloom in the brief mountain summer.

SKY FIGHTER

Fast and agile in the air, with a keen eye and rapid reflexes, the merlin is one of the top predators in the mountain food chain. It takes small birds, such as meadow pipits and snow buntings, in mid-air. In winter, as food sources dwindle, it extends its feeding range to include pastures, marshes, and coasts. Birds are particularly successful in mountain habitats because they can range over huge distances to look for food, and quickly fly to the lowlands to avoid bad weather and when winter arrives.

FUR AND FEET

Mammals that live on mountains cope with the cold by having an extra-thick coat of fur. They also have sturdy legs and flexible, rubbery hooves or paws to grip and clamber on steep slopes and over boulders. The mountain goat shows both of these adaptations. One advantage of mountain life is that predators are less common than on the lowlands, and more easily seen in the open landscape.

ELUSIVE PUMA

The puma is also called the cougar or mountain lion. It is as much at home on the slopes of the Adirondacks in the eastern United States as on the inhospitable, windswept shores at the tip of South America. It hides in rocky places and so it is seldom seen, even though it hunts by day as well as by night.

The desert life

THE FEATURES THAT CHARACTERIZE all deserts are a lack of water – less than 25 cm (10 in) of rain per year – and generally harsh conditions. Desert conditions are found in many parts of the world. Most deserts receive some rain, though it is highly unpredictable, and it is this potential source of water that makes life possible in this arid environment. Temperatures fluctuate widely, too. Many deserts are very hot in the day, but they can be extremely cold at night. Food is limited compared with most other habitats. However, a range of animals has adapted to living with a slight and irregular supply of water, and to conserving precious energy. By day, most desert animals hide from the searing sun in burrows or under rocks. They emerge to feed at night, when the air is cooler and damper.

Black band marks the position of the hood, which is extended when the cobra feels threatened

Diadem snake

Grey banded king snake

WAITING WITH VENOM
The red spitting cobra lurks in palm groves at oases in eastern Africa. When attacking its prey of small reptiles and mammals, the cobra bites to inject venom. Reptiles such as snakes, lizards, and tortoises do well in a desert habitat because they control their body temperature by gaining or losing heat from their surroundings. And compared to amphibians such as toads, with their permeable skin, reptiles are better suited to desert habitats because they have scaly skin to help them conserve moisture.

SPECIAL SNAKES
Like all snakes, the diadem snake uses its tongue to pick up scents from the air and the ground. The scents are then transferred to a sensory organ in the roof of the mouth which detects chemicals. The grey banded king snake has also adapted to desert life; its enormous eyes help it to spot prey during the night when it hunts to escape the daytime heat.

SHIP OF THE DESERT
The camel has long been used to carry people and goods across the sandy sea-like dunes, earning its name "ship of the desert". This mammal is admirably adapted to desert life with wide feet like sandshoes, thick fur to keep out heat and cold, and specialized body chemistry to conserve water.

*Sharp beak
to tear flesh*

Sting

Small pincers

*Wide tail helps
the hawk to
control gliding*

Protective scales

SLOW AND DRY
Scorpions that live in deserts are
especially venomous: this is so that they
do not waste precious energy fighting
in self-defence or subduing larger prey.
The hard body casing, or exoskeleton,
of creatures such as scorpions, spiders,
and insects cuts down loss of valuable
water from the body in the desert heat.

Powerful talons

EQUIPPED FOR THE KILL
The Harris' hawk is a top predator in the deserts
of North America. Seeking a diet consisting
mainly of reptiles, which may be thin on the
ground, each individual needs a vast area as its
hunting ground. The powerful talons grip the
squirming prey, and long legs with protective
scales keep the bird's body out of harm's way.

*Overlapping scales
allow for rapid and
agile movement*

179

Life at its richest

TROPICAL FORESTS, or jungles, are among the richest places on Earth for wildlife. This is partly because jungles grow where there is year-round warmth and moisture, and plenty of sunlight. These conditions provide an ideal habitat for all sorts of animals: in fact, there may be more animal species lurking in a few kilometres of jungle than there are in the whole of England. Because a tree provides different living conditions, from the leaf litter at its base to the highest branch, the types of animals that live in each part also vary greatly. The top of a tree, or canopy, takes most of the sunlight, while the forest floor is surprisingly gloomy because the dense foliage blocks out the light. Jungle animals are sustained by a continuous supply of food from blossoms and fruit all through the year. They are some of the most bizarre creatures to be found anywhere in the world.

FROG BEETLE
This Malayan frog beetle has powerful back legs for jumping, just like its amphibian namesake.

BEETLING ABOUT
Most beetles, including this leaf beetle, live in the forests of warm regions. There are over 300,000 beetle and weevil species – more than in any other insect family.

HIGH FLIER
Creatures which live in the high canopy have evolved accordingly. This flying gecko usually relies on its camouflage to hide in the leaves and branches. If spotted, it launches itself into the air and glides to safety. Loose flaps of skin along its body and limbs spread out to form a broad swooping surface.

BIRDS OF PARADISE
The splendid plumage of the male bird of paradise is used simply to attract a mate. Males gather in groups at traditional showing-off sites, called leks, in order to display. Some choose a high tree top and, as day breaks, give a colourful display, flashing their bright, iridescent plumage, and making loud calls. These birds live only in the tropical forests of Papua New Guinea, nearby islands, and northeastern Australia.

Wide scales along tail

Flaps make lizard wider and flatter for gliding

Scaly skin looks like lichen-covered bark

Long legs for running

Strong wings

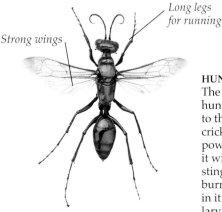

Webbing between toes

FLYING FROG
Reinwardt's flying frog is one of a small number of rainforest tree frogs that leap out of a tree to escape from a pursuer. The digits of their very large hands and feet are connected by webs of skin. During long, gliding leaps, these behave like parachutes.

HUNTING WASP
The electric-blue female hunting wasp cruises close to the forest floor, hunting for crickets. It grips its prey with powerful jaws and paralyses it with venom injected by its sting. It drags the insect into a burrow and lays a single egg in it so that, on hatching, the larva has food until it pupates.

SMASH THE FRUIT

The beaks of macaws and parrots are hooked and extremely powerful. They are adapted for piercing the tough husks and skins of fruits, and hooking out the juicy flesh and seeds from within. These birds live in tropical forests, although some species have become adapted to drier habitats.

FLYING SNAKE

This flying tree snake is one of five species from southeast Asia that can glide through the air. By raising its ribs upwards and outwards, the snake flattens its body and so manages to travel distances of up to 50 m (164 ft) from one tree to another. When it lands on the ground it resumes its usual shape.

FLYING DRAGON

The flying dragon is a type of lizard which has achieved its parachute shape in a different way to the flying gecko opposite. Six or seven pairs of very long rib bones covered with thin skin act as "wings". These are usually folded against the lizard's body, but open out so it can glide long distances.

MOST MASSIVE MOTH

The atlas moth is one of the largest of all butterflies and moths, with a wingspan of 30 cm (12 in). It survives in woods and forests across India and Sri Lanka to Malaysia, Indonesia, and China. But like other endangered jungle creatures, it is illegally collected and sold as an exotic pet, or even as a dead specimen.

Wing pattern and colours help males and females find each other

181

Animal classification

Almost every aspect of studying nature involves classification – placing living things into groups. Classification is constantly evolving as we learn more about living things. Most modern schemes start with five main groups, or kingdoms – monerans and protists (microscopic and single-celled animals), fungi, plants, and animals. The animal kingdom divides into two subgroups – the invertebrates and the vertebrates. These groups are divided into phyla which encompass animals with basic similarities in body structure, such as reptiles or mammals. Each phylum is then divided into classes, a class into orders, an order into families, a family into genera. Finally, each genus is divided into species. There are at least another 20 minor phyla, mostly of invertebrates which resemble worms or shellfish.

Invertebrates

Invertebrate species far outnumber the larger, more familiar vertebrates by at least twenty to one. The vast majority of invertebrates are insects, class Insecta, with more than one million described and catalogued species, and perhaps several million more yet to be identified. Insects, along with spiders, crabs and other crustaceans, and millipedes and centipedes, make up the largest phylum in the animal kingdom – the arthropods, or "jointed-legged" animals. Their basic common feature is a hard outer body casing, or exoskeleton, and legs which can be bent at the joints.

Sea anemone

Earthworm

Snail

Spider

Crab

Starfish

INSECTA
All insects belong to one class. They have six legs when adult, and most have two or four pairs of wings. The largest subgroup of insects is the beetles and weevils.

CNIDARIA
This is a sub-phylum of Coelenterata. Cnidarians have a jelly-like body and tentacles, and include jellyfish, corals, and sea anemones.

ANNELIDA
There are several phyla of worms. This one contains worms with many body segments, such as the earthworm.

MOLLUSCA
This phylum includes snails, slugs, octopuses, squids, mussels, and clams and similar shellfish. Most of them have a hard outer shell.

ARACHNIDA
Spiders, scorpions, and mites form this class in the phylum Arthropoda. Their basic feature is eight pairs of walking legs.

CRUSTACEA
This class of arthropods includes sea-living crabs, lobsters, prawns, shrimps, and barnacles, and a few land-dwellers such as woodlice.

ECHINODERMATA
Echinoderms are a phylum of sea-dwellers with a circular body plan, such as starfish, sea urchins, sea lilies, and feather stars.

Red admiral butterfly

Vertebrates

All vertebrates have a backbone, also known as a vertebral column, and a supporting skeleton inside the body, rather than around it as in many invertebrates. It is generally assumed that a structure as complicated as the backbone arose only once during evolution, so all vertebrates are related by their common ancestry. Most vertebrates are large, compared to invertebrates, with keen senses and a relatively large brain, and show variable and adaptable behaviour. The main phylum of vertebrates is Chordata, containing the classes of fish, amphibians, reptiles, birds, and mammals.

Lanner falcon

AVES
This class contains the birds. The key feature that makes a bird is its feathers. All birds are warm blooded, have a toothless beak, and forelimbs adapted as wings.

Tiger

Snake

Frog

Yellow cichlid

Dogfish

MAMMALIA
Mammals are warm blooded, like birds. They have a body covering of fur, apart from a few exceptions, and feed their babies on mother's milk.

REPTILIA
Reptiles have a dry, scaly skin, and most lay tough-shelled eggs. They include lizards, snakes, turtles and tortoises, and crocodiles and alligators.

AMPHIBIA
The amphibian class includes frogs, toads, salamanders, and newts. They have moist, scaleless skin, and lay jelly-covered eggs called spawn.

OSTEICHTHYES
This class of fish contains the bony fish, which number well over 20,000 species. They have a skeleton made of bone and most have flexible fins called ray fins.

CHONDRICHTHYES
Cartilaginous fish make up the second main class of fish. They have a skeleton made of cartilage, not bone. They all live in the sea and include sharks, skates, and rays.

The history of life

Paleozoic era

The history of the Earth is divided into major time periods called eras. In the first, the Precambrian era, life forms were mostly microscopic single cells. In the second, the Paleozoic era, larger and more complex animals evolved with shells, backbones, jaws, and legs. We know this from the evidence of fossils. Paleozoic means "ancient life".

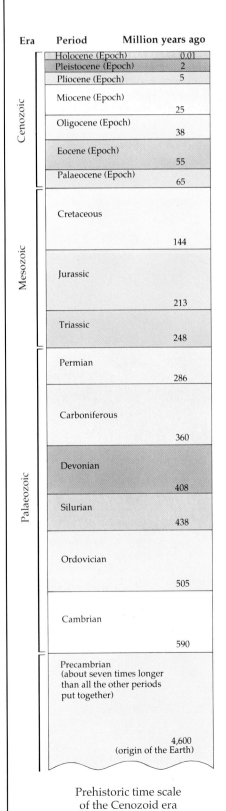

Era	Period	Million years ago
Cenozoic	Holocene (Epoch)	0.01
	Pleistocene (Epoch)	2
	Pliocene (Epoch)	5
	Miocene (Epoch)	25
	Oligocene (Epoch)	38
	Eocene (Epoch)	55
	Palaeocene (Epoch)	65
Mesozoic	Cretaceous	144
	Jurassic	213
	Triassic	248
Palaeozoic	Permian	286
	Carboniferous	360
	Devonian	408
	Silurian	438
	Ordovician	505
	Cambrian	590
	Precambrian (about seven times longer than all the other periods put together)	4,600 (origin of the Earth)

Prehistoric time scale of the Cenozoid era

TRILOBITE
Trilobites were distant cousins of crabs and lobsters. They all lived in the sea, appearing almost 600 million years ago but dying out by 200 million years ago.

NAUTILOIDS
Nautiloids and the similar ammonites were molluscs. Each had a body with many tentacles protruding from its coiled shell. Ammonites died out, but one nautiloid species, the nautilus, survives.

FISH
The first fish had no proper jaws or paired fins. This is a fossil of *Birkenia,* only 7 cm (3 in) long, which lived 420 million years ago.

AMPHIBIANS
The first land vertebrates were amphibians, which evolved during the Devonian period. The soft parts and skin are unusually well preserved in this fossil frog.

DINOSAURS
Over 1,000 species of dinosaurs have been identified from their fossils. They ruled the land for over 160 million years.

THE PREHISTORIC TIME SCALE
This chart shows the main eras and periods, plus the smaller time spans of the Cenozoic era, and how many millions of years ago they occurred. Fossils are dated from the type of rock in which they are embedded, the other fossils found with them, and by measuring the tiny amounts of radioactivity or magnetism in the fossil rock.

Mesozoic era

In the era of "middle life", the land was dominated by reptiles, and especially by dinosaurs. Reptiles also flourished in the seas and, as pterosaurs, in the air. Mammals had appeared, but they were insignificant. A mass extinction at the end of the Cretaceous period meant the end of many plants and animals.

BIRDS
The earliest bird, *Archaeopteryx*, lived nearly 150 million years ago. Bird bones are light, hollow, and fragile, and rarely fossilize.

ICHTHYOSAURS
These sharp-toothed, dolphin-shaped reptiles terrorized the seas for much of the Mesozoic era. Other Mesozoic marine reptiles included plesiosaurs and mosasaurs.

PLESIOSAUR
This fine fossil shows the limb bones of a plesiosaur which have turned to stone. Its legs were shaped like paddles for moving speedily through the water, yet still had the five "toes" common to most land vertebrates.

Cenozoic era

The era of "recent life", from 65 million years ago and into the present, has been marked by the rise of mammals to the dominant large animals on land, while birds have taken over the sky. But through all the eras, many groups of animals and plants have diversified. These include crustaceans, worms, fish, and insects.

HORSES
The earliest horse, *Hyracotherium*, was about the size of a pet cat. It lived in the forests of North America and Europe about 55 million years ago. Horses and other hoofed mammals form the ungulate group of mammals.

APES
The skull of the Miocene ape, *Proconsul*, has several similarities to today's chimps. Its blunt teeth indicate that it ate fruits and leaves. Apes, along with monkeys, lemurs, tarsiers, and bushbabies, form the primate group of mammals.

CATS
The sabre-toothed cat, *Smilodon*, had fearsome canine fangs to slash and slice at victims. It lived from about 1.6 million to only 8,000 years ago in North and South America. Cats, along with dogs, bears, raccoons, and mongooses, are in the carnivore group of mammals.

ELEPHANTS
Mammoths like this whole specimen, which was deep-frozen in Siberian ice, belonged to the elephant (proboscid) group of mammals.

GLYPTODONTS
The armoured *Glyptodon* lived in South America. Like many there, it became extinct when continental drift joined South to North America, and invading species from the North forced many South American mammals into extinction.

Skull of *Homo erectus*

EARLY HUMANS
Fossil skulls give a clear picture of how upright-walking, large-brained creatures called hominids evolved from an ape-like ancestor. Modern humans, *Homo sapiens*, may have appeared as little as 100,000 years ago. This skull belonged to *Homo erectus*, or upright man, an early ancestor of modern humans.

Glossary

ABDOMEN In insects, spiders, and crustaceans, the section of the body furthest away from the head. It is attached to the thorax. *See also* THORAX.

ANTENNA One of the paired sense organs, on the head of an invertebrate, used to feel or taste. *See also* INVERTEBRATE.

ASEXUAL REPRODUCTION A way of producing young which does not involve the joining of male and female cells. *See also* SEXUAL REPRODUCTION.

BLOOD A fluid that flows around the body, distributing nutrients and many other substances, and collecting wastes. The "blood" of invertebrate animals is more correctly known by other names, such as endolymph. *See also* NUTRIENT.

BONE A hard body substance that forms the skeleton or supporting framework of most vertebrate animals. It is made chiefly of minerals, especially calcium and phosphorus, and the protein collagen. *See also* SKELETON.

BRAIN A mass of interconnected nerves which is the body's control and coordination centre. Usually found in the head region, and in the skull of vertebrate animals.

CAMOUFLAGE The means by which an animal escapes the notice of predators, usually because it resembles its surroundings. *See also* DISRUPTIVE COLORATION.

CARNIVORE An animal that eats mainly other animals or their body parts. This term is usually used for animals that consume large chunks of animal flesh, such as lions and wolves. *See also* INSECTIVORE, PISCIVORE.

CARPAL To do with the part of a land vertebrate where the forelimb joins the hand or front foot, commonly called the wrist.

CARTILAGE A gristly substance in the body of animals. In some animals it forms the whole skeleton. In others it forms the coverings of the bones in a joint, and the framework of parts such as the ears. *See also* Bone, SKELETON.

CATERPILLAR The larva of a butterfly or moth. *See also* LARVA, METAMORPHOSIS.

CELL The microscopic unit that makes up most living things.

CHITIN A tough carbohydrate found in the external skeleton of insects, crustaceans, and spiders. *See also* SKELETON.

CHRYSALIS Another name which is given to the pupa of a butterfly or moth. *See also* PUPA, METAMORPHOSIS.

COLD-BLOODED ANIMAL An animal which cannot warm itself up, and therefore whose temperature depends on its surroundings. *See also* WARM-BLOODED ANIMAL.

DETRIVORE An animal that eats detritus, which includes the remains of dead animals, plants, and other living things. Sometimes called a scavenger or carrion-feeder.

DIGESTION The breakdown of food into nutrients, tiny parts small enough to be absorbed into the body. This usually happens by a combination of physical and chemical means.

DIGIT A finger, or toe, or another equivalent, such as a horse's hoof.

DISRUPTIVE COLORATION A means of camouflage whereby an animal's markings, such as bold stripes or spots, break up its body shape in order to confuse predators. *See also* CAMOUFLAGE.

DIURNAL An animal that is active during the day. *See also* NOCTURNAL.

ECOLOGY The study of how animals and plants live together and fit into the world around them.

ECOSYSTEM All the living things in a particular region such as a forest, lake, or river, as well as the soil, water, and non-living things they use. *See also* HABITAT.

EGG CELL A female sex cell, in animals and plants. *See also* SEXUAL REPRODUCTION.

EMBRYO A very young plant or animal, still inside the mother (in mammals), in an egg (in birds and reptiles), or in a seed (in plants).

ENAMEL The hard substance that covers the surface of teeth.

ENDOSKELETON A skeleton which is mainly on the inside of the body, and covered by softer parts such as muscles, as in ourselves and all vertebrates. *See also* SKELETON, EXOSKELETON.

EVOLUTION A very slow process of change that affects all living things. It can gradually change the characteristics of a species, and produce new species from existing ones. *See also* NATURAL SELECTION.

EXOSKELETON A skeleton which is mainly on the outside of the body, enclosing and encasing the softer body parts such as muscles, as in insects, crabs, and similar invertebrates. *See also* SKELETON, ENDOSKELETON.

FEMUR The main upper hindlimb bone in land vertebrate animals, eg. the human thigh. Also used to describe thigh-like structures in the legs of some invertebrate animals, such as insects.

FERTILIZATION In sexual reproduction, the stage at which male and female sex cells join together to form a single cell. *See also* EGG CELL, SPERM CELL, SEXUAL REPRODUCTION.

FIBULA One of two lower hindlimb bones in a land vertebrate animal, eg. the human shin. *See also* TIBIA.

FOOD CHAIN A food pathway that links different species in a community, passing down energy and nutrients from one organism to another. Each species is usually involved in several different food chains. The amount of energy passed on diminishes at each stage. *See also* FOOD WEB.

FOOD WEB A collection of interconnecting food chains in a community of living things. *See also* FOOD CHAIN.

FOSSIL The ancient remains of an animal or plant found preserved in rock.

FRUGIVORE An animal that eats mainly fruits, as well as other soft plant parts such as leaves and buds. *See also* GRAMNIVORE, HERBIVORE.

GILL Feathery structures in fish and other aquatic animals that extract oxygen from water for the purposes of respiration. *See also* RESPIRATION.

GRAMNIVORE An animal that eats mainly grains, seeds, nuts, and similar tough plant materials and fibres. *See also* FRUGIVORE, HERBIVORE.

HABITAT The environment needed by a particular species for its survival. *See also* ECOSYSTEM.

HEART A muscular body part that pumps blood or an equivalent body fluid, making it flow around the body. *See also* BLOOD.

HERBIVORE An animal that eats mainly plant material, especially leaves, buds, shoots, fruits and stems, and flowers. *See also* GRAMNIVORE, FRUGIVORE.

HIBERNATION A winter sleep-like state entered into by many small animals. During hibernation, the animal's body enters a state of torpor; its body temperature drops, and its metabolic rate slows down. *See also* METABOLISM.

HUMERUS The main upper forelimb bone in a land vertebrate animal, eg. the human upper arm. *See also* RADIUS, ULNA.

INSECTIVORE An animal that eats mainly insects. This diet may also include insect-like animals such as woodlice and millipedes. *See also* CARNIVORE.

INSTINCTIVE BEHAVIOUR A pattern of behaviour, such as a spider spinning its web, and a bird building its nest, that is inherited, or built into the animal's nervous system. *See also* NERVE CELL, NERVOUS SYSTEM.

INTESTINES Body parts, usually tube-like, that digest food and absorb it into the body. *See also* DIGESTION.

INVERTEBRATE An animal without a backbone (spinal column), such as a worm, spider, insect, or crab. *See also* VERTEBRA, VERTEBRATE.

KERATIN The protein that makes up skin, hair, fur, nails, hooves, and feathers. *See also* PROTEIN.

KIDNEY One of a pair of organs in an animal's body that removes waste from the blood and regulates its water content.

LARVA The young stage of an insect or other invertebrate, that looks quite different to its parent. *See also* METAMORPHOSIS.

LATERAL LINE A line of pressure sensors found along the side of a fish's body.

LIGAMENT A strong, flexible material that holds two bones together where they meet in moveable joints.

LIVER A body part that processes digested nutrients and other body chemicals, changing, storing, and releasing them according to the body's needs.

LUNG One of a pair of organs used by most vertebrates to breathe, and so exchange oxygen and carbon dioxide inside the body.

MANTLE In snails, oysters, and other molluscs, a layer of the body that makes calcium carbonate (chalk) and so builds up the shell.

METABOLISM All the chemical reactions that occur inside an organism. *See also* ORGANISM.

METAMORPHOSIS A complete change in body shape, such as when a caterpillar changes into a chrysalis and then into a butterfly.

MIGRATION A regular journey made by animals from one place to another.

MIMICRY Imitation of one living thing by another, in order to gain protection or hide from predators.

MINERAL A simple chemical, such as iron, which living things need to stay alive.

MOULTING The process of shedding skin, feathers, or fur.

MUSCLE A body part which can contract to move part or all of the body.

NATURAL SELECTION The process by which many different natural factors, from climate to food supply, steer the course of evolution. *See also* EVOLUTION.

NERVE CELL A cell specialized to conduct nerve impulses, also known as a neuron. *See also* NERVOUS SYSTEM.

NERVOUS SYSTEM The sensory and control system in most multicellular animals, consisting of a network of nerve cells. *See also* NERVE CELL.

NOCTURNAL An animal that is active at night and inactive during the day. *See also* DIURNAL.

NYMPH The young stage of an insect, such as a grasshopper.

OMNIVORE An animal that eats any kind of food, whether of plant, animal, or fungal origins. *See also* CARNIVORE, HERBIVORE.

ORGANISM Any living thing.

PARASITE Any organism that lives on or inside another (its host) and from which it takes food.

PECTORAL To do with the part of a land vertebrate animal where the forelimb joins the main body – the shoulder – or the equivalent position in a fish.

PELVIC To do with the part of a land vertebrate animal where the hindlimb joins the main body – the hip – or the equivalent position in a fish.

PHEROMONE A chemical released by one animal that has an effect on another. Insects, for example, use pheromones for many different functions, including marking trails, signalling alarm, or attracting members of the opposite sex.

PISCIVORE An animal that eats mainly fish. *See also* CARNIVORE.

PLANKTON The mass of microscopic plants and animals that floats near or at the surface of seas and lakes.

PREDATOR An animal that hunts other animals. *See also* PREY.

PREY The animals that are hunted and eaten by a predator. *See also* PREDATOR.

PROTEIN An organic compound which performs many functions in living things, from controlling chemical reactions to building structures such as hair.

PUPA The stage in the lifecycle of an insect during which the larva turns into an adult. *See also* CHRYSALIS, METAMORPHOSIS.

RADIUS One of the two lower forelimb bones in a land vertebrate animal, eg. the human forearm. *See also* ULNA.

RESPIRATION The process in living organisms of taking in oxygen from the surroundings and giving out carbon dioxide.

SEXUAL REPRODUCTION A way of producing young that needs two parents. One, the female, produces an egg cell while the other, a male, produces sperm.

SKELETON The supporting framework of an animal's body, which is usually jointed to allow movement. *See also* ENDOSKELETON, EXOSKELETON.

SKULL The set of fused bones or cartilages in the head of a vertebrate animal, which enclose the brain and house the main sense organs.

SPECIES A group of living things whose members can breed successfully with each other to produce fertile offspring, but who cannot breed with any other living things. *See also* ASEXUAL REPRODUCTION, SEXUAL REPRODUCTION.

SPERM CELL A male sex cell. *See also* EGG CELL, SEXUAL REPRODUCTION.

SPIRACLE A tiny air hole which allows air to enter an insect's trachae, or windpipe. It is surrounded by a ring of muscle which enables the spiracle to open and close.

STOMACH A body part which stores eaten food and begins the digestive process. *See also* DIGESTION.

SWIM BLADDER A balloon-like organ which contains gas. It allows a fish to be neutrally buoyant in the water, which means that it does not rise or sink. When a fish dives, it increases the amount of gas in its swim bladder so that the bladder will not be squashed by water pressure.

TADPOLE The larva of a frog or toad, which lives entirely in water and breathes through gills. *See also* GILL, LARVA, METAMORPHOSIS.

TARSAL To do with the part where the hindlimb of a land vertebrate animal joins the foot, commonly called the ankle. Also used to describe similar structures in invertebrate animals such as insects and spiders.

TENDON A tough cord or band of white inelastic tissue that attaches a muscle to a bone or some other part of an animal's body. *See also* BONE, MUSCLE.

THORAX In insects, spiders, and crustaceans, the middle part of the body. In insects, it carries the legs and wings. *See also* ABDOMEN.

TIBIA One of the two lower hindlimb bones in a land vertebrate animal, eg. the human shin. *See also* FIBULA.

ULNA One of the two lower forelimb bones in a land vertebrate animal, eg. the human forearm. *See also* RADIUS.

VERTEBRA One of the short, pillar-like bones that makes up the backbone. Together, the vertebrae form a hollow rod which contains and protects the spinal cord. Humans usually have 33 vertebrae. Some frogs have fewer than 12 vertebrae, while snakes can have over 400. *See also* VERTEBRATE.

VERTEBRATE An animal with a backbone (spinal column). There are five main groups of vertebrates: fish, amphibians, reptiles, birds, and mammals. *See also* INVERTEBRATE, VERTEBRA.

WARM-BLOODED ANIMAL An animal which makes its own heat by burning up food. It can be warm, even if its surroundings are cold. *See also* COLD-BLOODED ANIMAL.

Acknowledgments

Dorling Kindersley would like to thank:

David Pickering and Helena Spiteri for editorial assistance; and Alex Arthur, David Burnie, Dr. Barry Clarke, Juliet Clutton-Brock, Linda Gamlin, Theresa Greenaway, Miranda MacQuitty, Colin McCarthy, Dr. Angela Milner, Laurence Mound, Dr. David Norman, Steve Pollock, Ian Redmond, and Paul Whalley for contributing to the book.

Special photography
Geoff Brightling, Jane Burton and Kim Taylor, Peter Chadwick, Geoff Dann, Richard Davies (Oxford Scientific Films), Philip Dowell, Mike Dunning, Andreas von Einsiedel, Neil Fletcher, Frank Greenaway, Colin Keates and Harry Taylor (Natural History Museum), Dave King, Karl Shone, and Jerry Young; all the photographers at the British Museum.

Illustrators
Stephen Bull, Peter Chadwick, Will Giles, Mick Loates, Andrew Macdonald, Coral Mula, Richard Ward, Dan Wright, John Woodcock.

Model makers
Graham High, Jeremy Hunt

Index
Hilary Bell

Picture research
Fiona Watson

Every effort has been made to trace the copyright holders. Dorling Kindersley apologizes for any unintentional omissions and would be pleased, in such cases, to add an acknowledgment in future editions.

Picture credits
t=top b=bottom c=centre l=left r=right

Ardea 96tl / Jean-Paul Ferrero 110t, 126 br
Zedenek Berger 158c
G.I. Bernard 109tr
Biofotos / Heather Angel 97tr, 123tl, 156c, 157tr
Bridgeman Art Library / Alan Jacobs Gallery, London 26tr, 92tl, 92cl, 92c, 104tr, 112bl, 113tc
British Library 78bl
Prof. Edmund Brodie Jnr. 98bl, 140c
Danny Bryantowich 129bl
Zdenek Burian / Artia Foreign Trade Corp 162c
Dr. Barry Clarke 123tc
Bruce Coleman / Kim Taylor 55tr, 57tl, 64tl, 64cl, 78br, 79c / Michael Fogden 98clb, 112cl / A.J. Stevens 133tl, 133cl, 138cl / Jane Burton 160tl, 161tl, 177tl, 177cr
Mary Evans 26br, 30tr, 36b, 38tl, 38cl, 38bl, 40bl, 42tr, 42tl, 54tl, 64cr, 68tr, 71tl, 77cl, 88tl, 98tr, 106bl, 109bl, 110cb, 140tl, 141cr, 154tl, 160cl, 161cb
F.L.P.A / Leo Batten 69c
Giraudon 152tl
Robert Harding Picture Library / Philip Craven 21tr, 139t, 143tr
Eric and David Hosking 93tr, 93cr
Dave King / courtesy of National Motor Museum at Beaulieu 115tr
Kobal Collection 78t, 111cr
Bob Langrish 115tl
Mike Linley 98cl, 132tr
The Mansell Collection 36tl, 38clb, 43tl, 153tl
Military Archive and Research 128br Musée National d'Histoire Naturelle, Paris 158tr, 159tl, 166c
Natural History Museum, London 166br
N.H.P.A. / Peter Johnson 46cl, 72cr, 72bl, 73tr, 74tr, 114bl
Only Horses 115c
Naturhistoriska Riksmuseet 158cl
Oxford Scientific Film / Alistair Shay 56tl / Doug Perrine 61tl / Fred Baverdam 61cl / Jack Dermid 61cr / Zig Leszczynski 76tr, 89 bl, 124cl, 138bl, 156cl, 171bl, 172tl
Planet Earth / Brian Pitkin 60tl / Ken Lucas 60cr, 73br, 111bl, 155br, 172br, 179tl / Ian Redmond 75br
Science Photo Library / Sinclair Stammers 36c
David A. Hardy 165tl
Frank Spooner 142cl, 142bl, 142cbl
A. Tanner 113tr
Werner Forman Archive 111cr
Zefa / K. and H. Benson 63cl, 79bl, 114cl, 140crb
Dr. Eric Zimen 111tr